City Dwellers

Dr. Ernest W. Stokes, Jr.

**A Prosperity Message from Zion
for the New Covenant Generation
Who Dwell in Zion at Jerusalem**

ISBN-13: 978-1477499368
ISBN-10: 1477499369

Table of Contents

FOREWORD

I PETER 2:9 Ye are a chosen generation, a royal priesthood, a holy nation, God's Own people, that you may declare the wonderful deeds of Him who called you out of darkness into His marvelous light.

We are the chosen generation— the blessed children of God. And we have the right to dwell in Zion, the city of God— as *City Dwellers*, and enjoy the privileges of citizenship now. Many Christians go through life and never understand this life-changing truth.

Our enemy would like nothing better than to blindfold us from this wonderful truth and keep us captive for years, denying us of our rights and privileges as citizens of Zion. But, thanks to God the Father, He sent His Son Jesus to earth so we would know the truth. He set us free from bondage, and made the abundant life ours.

The Bible tells us much about the character and person of God, and relates the story of His people from the Creation through John's Revelation. The key for us is to apply its lessons to our own circumstances today. We can have the heritage of Jacob, the wisdom of Solomon, and can be *"more than conquerors"* as the Apostle Paul described God-fearing Christians— when we learn how to live victoriously on earth as a

New Covenant man, a new man in Christ, a triumphant believer.

Being "Baptized in the Spirit" and "baptized with fire" may seem puzzling to many Christians today. However, those of us who believe that the gifts of the Spirit are available to believers today know we should be living in victory. We cast off false teachings that such gifts disappeared with the Apostolic Age. All that is required is believing in God's Word— that our Lord Jesus chose and commissioned us as His disciples and royal priests. He wants us to be *City Dwellers*— living stones, offering spiritual sacrifices, that we may live with Him and the Father in Zion today, in this life and time.

So, no matter who we are in the world, we have all been called, declared and appointed by God for service in the Kingdom. Listening carefully, we can hear the voice of Jesus calling us to Zion to be His chosen bride. And God does not intend for His Son's bride to be defeated by the forces of evil while we sojourn on this earth. God intends that we be armed with the same armor made available to the early Christians who lived during the Apostolic Age. With this armor we win the battle— we dare not confront our enemy without it. All God wants us to do is "choose to be chosen". He will not force himself on anyone, but without making this choice, we cannot be justified as triumphant believers.

The Whole Armor of God

We must put on the *"whole armor of God"* to be victorious— to live as a "new man"— the "new covenant man" only Christ Jesus can make possible. To ensure that we can join the ranks of the eleven— as well as those who received the gifts of the Spirit at Pentecost, Jesus prayed the Father at the Last Supper to send us the Holy Spirit— to guide His chosen into all truth (John 15:26; 16:13).

The eleven disciples who remained on earth after the ascension of Christ Jesus received the Baptism in the Holy Spirit on the Day of Pentecost, together with other disciples of Jesus— about 120 in all. They were baptized with power just as many others in the early church would also be baptized during this Apostolic Age— instances of which are also recorded in the Book of Acts. What we must remember about this baptism is that Jesus was likewise empowered by the Father after He had been baptized with water by John the Baptist in the River Jordan. Yes, because Jesus prayed the Father that we may share all that He was given by the Father as joint heirs, this gift is available today to us— we are the present day *City Dwellers* (John 17:20).

City Dwellers— this is who we are. We are the "others" Jesus prayed for at the Last Supper. Listen. Do you hear the Holy Spirit's voice coming from deep inside of you, saying: "Child, your home is in Beulah Land. There you shall dwell— married to King Jesus, and from the City of your birth, you shall discharge the commission Jesus proclaimed for you while He was on earth— to achieve the Father's declared purpose."

We are today's chosen disciples and prophets. And, because of who we are, God wants to satisfy us with the abundant life on earth. And because we have the Name of Jesus, and His Word, which is above His Name, we can return to our homeland of Zion and find our way to experience this abundant life. Abraham believed God and his faith was reckoned to him as righteousness. Yet, despite his faith and that of all our Old Covenant heroes, they were never permitted to return to Zion, their homeland. They had no Savior, but because we belong to Christ Jesus, God blesses our going into Zion to renew our strength and our coming out again to find pasture in Jerusalem. We are God's New Covenant Generation, called to serve— born of His Spirit and washed in His blood, called out of darkness into His marvelous light. God desires that we prosper— enjoying the life Jesus died for us to have as His empowered vessels, ensuring that His Word accomplishes His purpose.

1

Who Do We Say We Are?

Genesis 1:27-28   God created man in His Own image, in the image of God He created him; male and female He created them. And God blessed them, and God said to them, "Be fruitful and multiply, and replenish the earth and subdue it; and have dominion over the fish of the sea and the birds of the air, and over every living thing that moves upon the face of the earth."

John 4:23-24   "The hour is coming, and now is, when the true worshipers will worship the Father in spirit and truth, for such the Father seeks to worship Him. God is Spirit, and those who worship Him must worship Him in spirit and truth."

We are children of God— spirits, just as He is Spirit. In the beginning, God created man in His Own image and after His likeness— male and female, to be fruitful and multiply, to replenish the earth and subdue it, and to have dominion over the fish of the sea, the birds of the air, and over every living thing that moves upon the earth (Genesis 1:26-28). God commanded man to have dominion on earth. How great this blessing. Our spirit was created in the image and likeness of God, we were created in His perfection— for a purpose, to have dominion over all living things. From the dust of the earth God made man a body of flesh— just the right composition of matter needed to live on the earth; placed his perfect spirit in this body and breathed the breath of life into him; and gave him a soul with a free will capable of expressing feelings and making his own decisions about right and wrong. Yes, in the same way, God blessed each of our spirits when He created us in Zion— in His identical image and likeness. And, from the union of Adam and Eve until today, God has made each of our bodies from the matter of the earth's crust, but as distinctively unique vessels.

We Are on Earth to Receive
and Discharge Our Assignments

The most important thing for us is to believe who we are. Luke 1:28-38 records the visit by the angel of the Lord with Mary to tell her she was to birth Jesus. We cannot imagine what Mary must have felt when the angel said to her, *"Mary, the Lord God has found favor in you, and you shall birth a son from your womb named Jesus, to Whom the Lord God shall give the throne of David to reign over the House of Jacob forever."* Highly favored and blessed among women? *"But I am a virgin,"* she told the angel perplexed— only to hear him respond, *"The Holy Spirit shall come upon you, and the power of the Most High God shall overshadow you — for with God nothing shall be impossible".* We know in verse 38 that Mary received and accepted what God chose her to do— acknowledging who she was in her acceptance, *"Behold the handmaid of the Lord*

6

God; let it be unto me according to Your Word."

We Must Decide to Receive, Accept and Acknowledge God's Gifts

Mary made a decision to receive, accept, and acknowledge God's gift of the Christ child. Although she was a virgin, she never first consulted Joseph to whom she was betrothed; nor did she discuss her decision first with her cousin Elizabeth with whom she was very close. She did it by her own volition. God's gifts must be received, accepted, and Our Father must be acknowledged as the giver— by each individual believer. Although we all belong to the body of Christ Jesus, all of us profess to be *City Dwellers*, and all of us worship in the church sanctuary as a corporate body, each individual believer's faith in God's Word must be professed by the believer's mouth; and each action performed by the believer's actual doing of the thing required to activate his or her faith. Productive faith requires action on our part (James 2:17).

"Be Fruitful and Multiply"

Each one of us must ask, "Who do I say I am?" God wants us to know that we, like Mary, are blessed and highly favored. He is pleased with us and has chosen us for duty in the Kingdom. So we ask Him, "Father, what do you desire me to do for the Kingdom while I'm here on earth?" We have part of the answer in Genesis 1:28 as we hear God declaring His blessing upon mankind, saying to all of us, *"Be fruitful and multiply, and fill the earth and subdue it; and have dominion over the fish of the sea, the birds of the air, and over all living things that move upon the face of the earth."* But until we hear His voice, calling us by name, we may not be able to apply Genesis 1:28 to our own circumstances. John 10:27-28 answers that question, too. We hear the voice of Christ Jesus speaking directly to us through the Holy Spirit who resides in us, saying, *"My sheep hear My voice, and I know them — and they follow Me. And I give them eternal life."* Examine the answer in Romans 8:29-30 closely and we know why we hear His voice: God declared that we would hear Him calling us because He chose us before we were born to be conformed to the image of His Son— that He might be the firstborn among many brethren. Colossians 1:15-20 confirms this: Christ Jesus is the image of the invisible God, the first-born of all creation; for in Him all things were created, in heaven and on earth, visible and invisible— all things were created through Him and for Him. He is before all things, and in Him all things hold together. He is the Head of the body, the church; He is the beginning, the first-born from the dead, that in everything He might be pre-eminent. For in Him the fullness of God was pleased to dwell; and through Him to reconcile to himself all things, whether on earth or in heaven, making peace by the blood of His cross.

Jesus Has Chosen
City Dwellers as His Disciples

Matthew 5:1-2 Seeing the multitudes, Jesus went up into a mountain. And when He was set His disciples followed Him— and He opened His mouth and taught them, saying...

Christ Jesus taught us to hear the Word of God coming forth in His voice when He opened His mouth. Two important points must be made here. First, note that only the disciples of Jesus heard Him when He preached the *Sermon on the Mount*. His sermon was meant not for the multitudes who may have heard of Him or had become somewhat fascinated by Him. It was by intent and probably quite a climb that Jesus chose to go up into the mountain. He knew that only those who were His disciples or who yearned to be among them would follow Him up into the mountain. Those who followed Him were the ones who believed in Him and were eager to listen to the words of wisdom and healing that came forth from His mouth.

Jesus Commissioned Us to
Proclaim the Good News of the Gospel

This is not to say that the reference in verse 1 to "His disciples" meant only the "twelve", since the gospel accounts indicate that Jesus probably delivered His *Sermon on the Mount* before all of the twelve had been chosen. We also know that references in the gospels to "disciples of Jesus" often included more than the twelve— including as a general rule all those who believed in Jesus as the Son of God by the words of their testimony. We are His disciples today.

God Speaks the Words
That Come Forth from Our Mouth

The other important point that must be emphasized in the introduction to the *Sermon on the Mount* is that this very sermon was prophesied centuries before— even the words that came out of Jesus' mouth. The prophet Nahum prophesied, *"Behold, on the mountains the feet of Him who brings good tidings, who proclaims peace"* (Nahum 1:15); and the prophet Isaiah also when he wrote, *"Get you up to a high mountain, O Zion, herald of good tidings"* (Isaiah 40:9). Jesus did just that. When He was set, and those who were to come had come, Jesus opened His mouth to teach the disciples who followed Him up into the mountain. And when He did, the Holy Spirit caused the Word of God to come forth from His mouth. Christ Jesus was sent by His Father to preach the gospel of peace and bring glad tidings of good things. He is the one whose feet trod up onto the mountain to deliver the *Sermon on the Mount* (Matthew 5, 6, 7). And, as we study the sermon carefully, we see that the prophet Isaiah prophesied what Jesus would preach (Isaiah 61:1-3); and with it, Jesus completed what he had declared in the synagogue at Nazareth after He had returned from the wilderness (Luke 4:18-21).

The Apostle Paul teaches on this very point in Romans 10:13-17, explaining how this sermon is intended to be preached by His disciples, *"Whosoever shall call upon the Name of the Lord shall be saved. But how shall they call on Him in Whom they have not believed? And how shall they believe in Him of Whom they have not heard? And how shall they hear without a preacher? And how shall they preach unless they are sent? As it is written, how beautiful are the feet of them that preach the gospel of peace, and bring glad tidings of good things. But they have not all obeyed the gospel; for as the prophet Isaiah asked, 'Who has believed our report?' So then, faith comes from hearing and hearing by the Word of God."* Reading the second part of Isaiah 40:9 again, we see that his prophecy suddenly applies directly to us, *"Get you up to a high mountain, O Zion, herald of good tidings. Lift up your voice with strength, O Jerusalem, herald of good tidings, lift it up, fear not; say to the cities of Judah, 'Behold your God'."* Thus, when we read this verse and Romans 10:15 together, we can readily see that we are Zion and Jerusalem. And God blesses our feet as we proclaim good tidings to all those who desire to hear it— wherever our feet shall trod; as we walk in the way, in the light of His countenance, the path that His light shines upon (Psalm 89:15 & 119:105; John 14:6).

The Righteous Shall Live by Faith

HEBREWS 10:38   But My righteous one shall live by faith; if he shrinks back, My soul has no pleasure in him.

Faith is the key to our success in this life. If we can envision the things we hope for appearing on earth, we are using our spiritual senses. Seeing things that are not indicates that we are able to see things in the spirit realm. If we can hear things that are not of this world, we will know that our spirit is somewhere other than on earth. Sometimes we might smell something so sweet that we know it is not of this world. It's not as though we have left earth— that is, our bodies are still here. But our spirit man is a traveler. City Dwellers, our home is in Mount Zion— we are only sojourning in Jerusalem. We are on a mission— to do what we have been assigned to do by Christ Jesus, so that Jerusalem on this side of the threshold can be restored to become a mirror image of the heavenly city of Zion. This is our charge. When we can believe that things exist that are not, God sees our faith at work— and He credits it to us as our righteousness (Romans 4:24; James 2:17).

2

Tenets of the Full Gospel Christian Faith

God Desires to Draw All Men Unto Himself

JOHN 12:32 "If I am lifted up, I will draw all men unto Myself."

We know who God declares we are. The Apostle Peter's confession in Matthew 16:16, *"You are the Messiah, the Son of the Living God,"* is ours, too, so we surely know who Jesus is. We confess, "Jesus is Lord" (Romans 10:9). But who do we say we are? When we can answer that question fully, we are ready to make a total commitment to the Master — to serve Him until the end of our life here on earth; and, as He desires, in the age to come — the Age of Jubilee. When we can say that we are *City Dwellers*, we understand the Father's plan for the salvation of mankind — He gave Jesus to the world, that whosoever believes in Him shall never perish, in this age or the next (John 3:16).

In order for the world to receive His only begotten Son, Christ Jesus, we have a job to do — a story to tell to the nations. If we will lift up the Name of Jesus, the words of Jesus, and the person of Jesus,

He will draw all men unto Himself. And He will open the door to the Father's throne room and the abundant life in this age. If we are truly His disciples, His ministers, His ambassadors to the nations, it will require us to affirm certain tenets of our Christian faith to help us identify ourselves as spirit beings, disciples of Christ Jesus— His ambassadors on earth, and the reality that we dwell in Zion and Jerusalem. There are 25 Tenets given here to help us establish who we believe we are. Once this fact is firmly established in our heart, we can be about our Father's business— to draw all men unto Himself, in Christ Jesus. We dare not let Our Father's Word return to Him void. His Word will be fulfilled. We have the Father's promise, the Holy Spirit's declaration, and Jesus' words of assurance that He will prosper each willing vessel who enables it to be fulfilled (Isaiah 55:11).

25 Prosperity Tenets

ISAIAH 55:11 "My Word which goes forth from my mouth will accomplished that which I have purposed it to do; and prosper the thing in which I sent it.

(1) We believe that we are created in the spiritual image and after the spiritual likeness of God the Father and God the Son; and, as spirits, born of their Spirit in Zion, we have been commanded by God to be fruitful and multiply — the fruit of our bodies; faith, which He has credited to us as our

righteousness; and the light of the fruit of the Holy Spirit working in us to produce love, joy, peace, patience, kindness, goodness, faithfulness, gentleness, self-control, against such there is no law. And, with a precious Savior in Christ Jesus, whose blood cleanses us from all unrighteousness, the Holy Spirit ever present in us as our comforter, the Word as our source book to meditate upon day and night, and our word of testimony, as we lift Him up, we shall overcome evil as He draws all men to Himself (Genesis 1:26-28; John 12:32; Galatians 5:22-23; Revelation 12:11).

(2) We believe that, as spirits, we were given spiritual dominion over the fish of the sea, the birds of the air, and over all living things that move upon the earth— to be used for the common good of our brethren in Christ; and, as declared by Our Creator to be our inheritance on earth and in Zion, the promised land allocation established by God the Father is ours (Genesis 1:28; Deuteronomy 3:1-22; Joshua 12-23).

(3) We believe that through the crucifixion and resurrection of our Lord Jesus, the Son of God, by the blood of the everlasting covenant, Jesus paid the ransom for our release from captivity, redeemed us from death, restored our dominion Adam had lost to satan, and now sits at the

Father's right hand where He makes intercession for us (Hebrews 13:20; Romans 8:34).

(4) We believe that Our Lord Jesus has baptized us in the Holy Spirit and with fire; and has given us His power and authority on earth to go wherever He asks us to go, baptizing in the Name of the Father, Son and Holy Spirit— and teaching and discipling the nations of Abraham as He commanded (Matthew 3:11 and 28:18-20).

(5) We believe that we can and will do the things that our Lord Jesus did when He was on earth— even the greater things that He declared for us and commanded us to do (John 14:12 &16:14-15; Luke 9:1-2).

(6) We believe that our Lord Jesus has made us kings and priests unto the Father to reign as His vessels on earth (I Peter 2:5-9; Revelation 5:10).

(7) We believe that we have been empowered by the Holy Spirit to be witnesses on earth for our Lord and Savior Christ Jesus, proclaiming what He has done for us; and that He has taught us how to profit (Isaiah 48:17; Matthew 28:18-20 & 10:27; Acts 1:8).

(8) We believe that Christ Jesus has given us His authority and Word of Power, and the use of His Name, to teach and disciple the nations of Abraham, preach the Word of Truth, communicate

the Baptism in the Holy Spirit, exercise power and authority over devils, cure diseases, and heal the sick (Luke 9:1-2 and 10:1, 9; John 14:14; Acts 1:8; Hebrews 1:3).

(9) We believe that no weapon formed against us can prosper when we put God first in our lives; that we are established in the land of promise; and that He will meet our every need and grant us our heart's desires as we carry out the work of the Kingdom of God on earth in victory (Isaiah 54:17; Matthew 6:33; Psalm 37:4).

(10) We believe that the words of our Lord Jesus will never pass away, and the gifts of the Holy Spirit are for today; and that we have received His gifts to minister to and enjoy fellowship with our brethren (Matthew 24:35; I Corinthians 12:7).

(11) We believe that God the Father has given us the glory on earth that He gave Christ Jesus; and has made us perfectly one in Him and Jesus, and them one in us, to be all we can be on earth now and forever — in the spirit of oneship (John 17:21-24).

(12) We believe that we can be with our Lord Jesus where He is in Zion now— during this Age, and in the Age to come; and, because Jesus made a Way for the redeemed, we have direct access to God the Father in His throne room today (John 10:9-10).

(13) We believe that the Father has given us a land of promise for which we did not labor, cities which we did not build, and vineyards we eat of today which we did not plant; and that both He and Christ Jesus have come and made their home in us that we may have their presence and assurance of our authority and power over this land, these cities and vineyards now and forever (Joshua 24:13; John 14:23).

(14) We believe that every place on this earth that the sole of our feet tread upon has been given to us for the common good — and, as allocated, for ourselves as our inheritance (Joshua 1:3-4).

(15) We believe that Christ Jesus has given us the Holy Spirit to preach the good news to the poor; heal the brokenhearted; proclaim liberty to those in captivity, opening of the prison gates to those who are bound, victory to those who mourn in Zion, and today as the acceptable year of Our Lord (Isaiah 61:1-2; Psalm 107).

(16) We believe that our faith in God's Word can move mountains; and enables us to bless ourselves, our loved ones and the brethren in the Body of Christ Jesus (Genesis 12:3; Mark 11:23).

(17) We believe that God has taught us how to profit and enjoy the fullness of His treasury in Zion, in this Age; that what is impossible with man is possible with God — and the abundant life Jesus promised is ours, even the hundredfold return can be ours as we plant His Word firmly in our hearts (Isaiah 48:17; Malachi 3:10-12; Mark 4:20 & 10:27-30; John 10:10).

(18) We believe that we have been given the full armor of God, including the ability to pray in the spirit with a prayer language known only to God — for daily communications with God the Father, Christ Jesus, and the Holy Spirit; to intercede on behalf of others; and to submit petitions; confront and stand firm against the powers of evil (Ephesians 6:10-18; Mark 16:17).

(19) We believe that we are established in the land of promise; that we can bind the strong man, plunder his house, and pull down his stronghold; and when we catch him in the act of stealing the things God has given to us for our enjoyment in this life, some of which are already in his house, he will be required to repay us sevenfold for every thing he has stolen from us, even those imperishable things such as our joy and peace; that we can remove and dispossess him from the land God has given us (Proverbs 6:31; Mark 3:27; II Cor. 10:4).

(20) We believe that we can mount up to the Holy City of Zion in the Spirit on a regular basis where Jesus awaits our arrival; that the Holy Spirit takes us up where Christ Jesus meets us on the highway; that Jesus walks and talks with us along the highway for the redeemed, while he leads us into His Garden, onto Mount Zion, through the city gates— along city streets; and into the courts of our Father, into His temple— even into His throne room, where we are strengthened, enjoy a discussion with our Father; and we go out again, back down to Jerusalem where we find good pasture (Isaiah 35:8-9; Song of Solomon 6:2-3, 11-12; Ezekiel 40:2 & 41:1; John 10:9).

(21) We believe that what seems impossible with man is possible with God— that all these blessings are ours now, on this earth, and forever in Zion with God the Father, Jesus and the saints (Luke 18:27; John 10:10).

(22) We believe that Our Risen Lord Jesus conquered death, is now in Zion, seated at the right hand of God the Father, where He awaits our arrival; and that we who overcome evil may sit with Him at His right hand now and forever (Acts 2:33; Eph. 1:20; Psalm 110:1).

(23) We believe that we are His kings and priests on earth today; that we are living stones, a spiritual house with Christ Jesus as the

cornerstone, a holy priesthood— to offer up spiritual sacrifices, acceptable to God by Christ Jesus; and that we have presented our bodies on the altar of God, as a living sacrifice; and that Christ Jesus has given us ministerial gifts so that we may continue His ministry on earth (Genesis 28:17, 22; I Kings 18:30-38; Rev. 5:10; Romans 12:1; I Peter 2:5-9; I Corinthians 12:28-30).

(24) We believe that we are willing New Covenant vessels to receive the Word, and to carry out the commission that Christ Jesus has given us; that we have been predestined to cause our Father's Word to be performed on earth— and that He will prosper us (Phil. 6:19; Isaiah 55:11).

(25)We believe that the ever-present Holy Spirit of the Father and the Son, Whom Jesus sent us and Who abides in us, has given us spiritual gifts, empowering us to use them courageously for the common good of the brethren, and to live the abundant life here on earth (John 10:10 and 14:12-23; I Corinthians 12:4-11).

3

Our Citizenship Requirements

DEUTERONOMY 5:6-7   "I am the Lord thy God, which brought thee out of Egypt, from the house of bondage. Thou shall have none other gods before me."

LUKE 10:27 "You shall love the Lord your God with all your heart, and all your soul, and all your strength, and all your mind; and your neighbor as yourself."

MICAH 6:8 And what does the Lord require of you, but to do justice and love kindness; and to walk humbly with Him.

God's Law includes the Ten Commandments, statutes, and ordinances God gave to Moses; and is recorded for us in the first five books of the Old Testament. God the Father does everything in perfection.   Psalm 19:7-10 describes the character and benefits of the Law of the Lord; and within His Law we see the love of God poured out for us.

You might say, "The Ten Commandments are obligatory."   While strict obedience is not required for salvation, provided we confess our sins, how can we continue to sin and expect to be justified before God?

The Ten Commandments Teach Us Obedience and Trust

Any discussion of the responsibilities of our citizenship in Zion should begin with the words, obedience and trust. Our perfect obedience to God, His commandments, ordinances and statutes cannot be compromised. It is disastrous for believers who are under the impression that since Jesus came and died on the cross, they are no longer under the Law. They dare to believe that keeping the Law, God's Commandments and Statutes— His Holy Word that Christ Jesus embodied while He was here in the flesh, is somehow no longer in effect. Not so. Yes, our violations of God's Word may be forgiven by the Father because of the sacrifice our Lord Jesus made for us at Calvary. But when we sin, any man or woman of God should instantly feel shame; and can't wait to confess it before Him and our High Priest Christ Jesus, our Lord and Savior. Only because He bought our release from the captivity of evil with His Own perfect blood sacrifice made for each of us are we assured of our Father's forgiveness— and, therefore, we are saved to spend eternity with Him and the Father in Zion. Because we have been redeemed from the curse and our sins forgiven, the devil cannot accuse us of something already blotted out. When we sin and ask forgiveness, He is faithful and just, and will forgive us and cleanse us from all unrighteousness (I John 1:9). True, the blood of Christ Jesus covers over our sins upon our humbling ourselves before the Father, asking Him for forgiveness, and making a commitment to repent in all our ways. Therefore, because Jesus sacrificed himself for our sins, our disobedience to the Law no longer bars us from Zion.

But is the Law obsolete for today? No, the Law has not been negated. Ask yourself, "What kind of life would we live here on earth if there were no law?" How can we expect to please our Father if we are disobedient to or disinterested in complying with His Law? How can we expect to inherit the abundant life or the hundredfold return Jesus came to give us without our regard for the Law? The truth is that if we continue sinning after we have given our life to our Lord Jesus, repenting of our sins— only to continue in our sinful habits and ways, we expose ourselves to endless attacks of death, destruction and deprivation.

Hebrews 10:26 warns us that if we sin deliberately after receiving the knowledge of the truth, there remains no sacrifice for our sins; and we miss the blessings of faithful Abraham as given to his descendants (Genesis 12:3). We shall bless ourselves as the new man in Christ Jesus only by making certain that we are right with God. Our obedience must be shown to our God.

A Perfect Law Was Given by God to Reconcile Man to Himself

> PSALM 19:7-11 The Law of the Lord is perfect, converting the soul; the testimony of the Lord sure, making wise the simple, the statutes of the Lord are right, rejoicing the heart; the commandments of the Lord are pure, enlightening the eyes. The fear of the Lord is clean, enduring forever; the judgements of the Lord are true and righteous altogether. More to be desired are they than gold, yea, than much fine gold; sweeter also than honey and the honeycomb. Moreover, by them is thy servant warned; and in keeping them there is great reward.

When the Law was given to Old Covenant people, it became essential that total obedience to God would be required in order for sinful man to regain God's favor. Thus, the Law became the Law of Sin and Death; and the punishment for disobedience in this life banished the soul of mankind from God's presence— on earth and in heaven. The devil and accuser of mankind made certain that no man or woman could enter Zion because of the sinful nature of their soul while on earth. When Jesus came, the Law of Sin and Death which once condemned man to death because of unforgiven sin, became the Law of the Spirit of Life. The Apostle Paul's letter to the Romans confirmed this truth, saying in Romans 8:1-2, *"There is now no condemnation for those who are in Christ Jesus — for the Law of the Spirit of Life* has set us free from the Law of Sin and Death. Thus, the perfection of God is seen in His Law – and His Testimony as given to us by the prophets." When we read Psalm 19:7-11 and Micah 6:8, the Law becomes a measure by which man can be reconciled to God the Father. It ceases to be a Code of Conduct and an instrument of punishment for our disobedience. His commandments, His ordinances, and His testimony by the prophets constitute His Law; and represent God's plan for restoring man to good standing with Him. As a result of our obedience to the Law, the abundant life here on earth is available to us in this life. The key to this life that Jesus came to give us (John 10:10) is possible when we pursue God's perfect will. How can we enjoy the abundant life here on earth if we are not walking in His perfect will? How can we enjoy the best of everything in this lifetime without honoring the Most High God and showing Him our obedience to His Law?

"Not One Jot or Title Shall Pass from the Law"

MATTHEW 5:18   "For verily I say unto you, till heaven and earth pass away, not one jot or tittle shall pass from the Law, till all be fulfilled."

MATTHEW 22:35-40 Then one of the Pharisees, a   lawyer asked him a question, tempting him, and saying, "Master, which is the greatest commandment in the Law?" Jesus said unto him, "Thou shall love the Lord your God with all your heart, all your soul, and all your mind.   This is the first and great commandment; and a second is like it, you shall love your neighbor as yourself. On these two commandments depend all the Law and the prophets."

Before Adam's fall from grace, there was no Law nor was there a need for the Law. Man had no knowledge of evil. The need for the Law arose when Adam, who had the best of everything God could give him in the Garden of Eden, including dominion over all creatures of the earth, ate of the forbidden fruit of the Tree of the Knowledge of Good and Evil— despite God's warning that he would die on that very day (Genesis 2:15-17).

Thereafter man knew evil— and that it was the opposite of good, but because Adam chose evil over good, he and all his descendants in every Old Covenant Generation lost favor with God. God pronounced His punishment upon Adam and Eve (Genesis 3:17-19), banishing them from the Garden of Eden where they enjoyed daily communion with God, and had all the sustenance they would ever need— and God banished them from Zion and all of God's Holy Mountain; and a curse fell upon them both— which separated them from God.

God created Adam as part of Himself but gave him a free will.. He loved Adam so much that He did not want the devil to ever invade his soul. But from the day he fell away from God, after he and Eve were banished from the garden, the devil's curse fell upon them. God initiated the practice of animal sacrifices to purify them of their sins. This practice continued, both before and after the flood, but no animal's blood was found sufficient to wash away or blot out sin— because when Adam sinned, everything he touched became impure; and mankind remained accursed. God allows us to go our own way if we insist. The only requirement for us to inherit eternal life is our acceptance of Christ Jesus as our Lord and Savior. But we can be living in eternity today, the abundant life is available to us today, as we humble ourselves before our Most High God.

Learn What Pleases the Lord

EPHESIANS 5:10 Try to learn what pleases the Lord, find out what He desires to see in us.

ISAIAH 55:11 And God said, My Word that goes forth from My mouth will not return to Me void; it shall accomplish what I have purposed, and prosper in the thing that received it.

The best way to learn what pleases God the Father is to seek His Word and His counsel. In the beginning God showed us everything He created— and it was good. He wants His children to continue "creating" good things in His Name. As Genesis 1:31 records for us, God declared all such good things into existence; and He saw them as very good. But Adam surrendered the perfect earth and all its beauty to satan, requiring God to send His Perfect Son to earth, in the flesh, to show His true disciples how to retrieve the good things He had proclaimed for them in the beginning. Christ Jesus, who died on the cross for us so that the abundance of the perfect earth could again be made perfect in and through us, became the Pioneer and Perfecter of our faith so that these good things are ours (Hebrews 12:2).

Developing an Excellent Spirit

DANIEL 6:3   Then this Daniel was preferred above the presidents and prince, because an excellent spirit was in him; and the king thought to set him over the whole realm.

God has given the New Covenant Generation such a bounty of blessings that we are unable to count them. Ask yourself, "What will it take for me to develop an excellent spirit like that of the prophet Daniel?" We have quite an advantage over Daniel— we enjoy the constant comfort of the Holy Spirit. Let's read Matthew 6:33 first to hear Jesus speaking to us: *"Seek ye first the Kingdom of God and His righteousness, and all these things shall be added unto you."*

We need to know how to develop such an excellent spirit so we can accomplish the Kingdom work God has declared for us— so we can receive, accept and experience the things we hope for— indeed, the abundant life in this age. So, as we look at what God requires of *City*

Dwellers, it helps to determine what profits us and what hinders us as we discharge the commission Jesus has given us as His disciples. We know that He expects us to let our light so shine before men that they will see our good works and glorify our Father in heaven (Matthew 5:16). What many of us fail to understand is that He is talking about works of faith. Faith in what? His Word. This brings us back to trust. We must trust in His Word to accomplish His purpose in us.

Daniel's Prophecy Is for the New Covenant Generation

We know that the prophet Daniel prophesied that the saints of God would inherit the Kingdom of God and possess it forever (Daniel 7:18). As depicted in the Book of Daniel, probably written during the Babylonian captivity, the Old Covenant Generation awaited the arrival of a king who would restore their physical dominion on earth and give them hope for divine prosperity.

Then as now God searches the hearts of men and women to find those whose heart is right toward Him; He needs faithful servants to lead His people; and anoints whosoever He chooses (II Chron. 16:9).

What Is Required for Us to Experience the Abundant Life Today?

Before God can allow us to share His family name and heritage, use His Beloved Son's Name, and go about doing the family business that He has declared for us to do, it really is a matter of showing Him the honor and praise He so rightly deserves as our Creator — the one who loves us so much that He gave us a Savior in His Son, Christ Jesus. It's not enough for us to merely declare who we are; we must be willing vessels who will remain obedient to His commandments, and trust in His Word to accomplish what He desires to give us — to meet our needs and give us the desires of our heart (Matthew 6:33; Psalm 37:4). A test of the honor in how we regard God the Father is the 5th Commandment (Deuteronomy 5:16).

Honoring Our Parents

When we hold our own parents who birthed us and love us in high esteem — as well as our grandparents and any others who may have contributed to our upbringing, love them, and show them the respect they deserve, we are showing God that we know the meaning of the word, honor. By our display of love, respect, obedience and trust for them, not only do we show our parents how much we appreciate what they have done for us; we show God that we know how to honor Him and we do it willingly. He wants first place in our lives — and with it, our love, honor, obedience and trust. And we learn by doing it daily. No wonder this commandment carries with it His promise of our prolonged life to serve Him on this earth.

Following in the
Footsteps of Our Lord Jesus

Our Father intends for all His children to follow in his Son's footsteps. We must also be willing to accept our baptism by fire. Remember: Jesus is our Baptizer. Let's be certain that we are equipped with spiritual weaponry to displace the strong man who today dares to walk upon the land God gave us (Ephesians 6:10-18; Joshua 1:2-3). This is a requirement for all believers. But we must be in the Spirit to counsel with God the Father in His throne room where Jesus sits at His right hand (Psalm 110:1). Jesus made all this possible, saying in John 10:9, *"I am the Door; if anyone enters by Me, he will be saved, and will go in and come out and find pasture."* The Holy Spirit will take us and Jesus will greet us there when we really desire to "go up" to Zion.

When Our Discipleship Pleases God

MICAH 6:8 He has shown you, O man, what is good; and what does the Lord require of you, but to do justice, and to love kindness, and to walk humbly with your God?

We please God when we walk humbly with Him. Micah's prophecy assures us that our hearts must be right with God to receive the best things He has reserved for us in Zion— things God wants us to have as His obedient children whom He made in His Own image. We are the chosen generation— His children and joint heirs of the Kingdom with Jesus. God earnestly desires to profit us. But first we must realize that we are spiritual beings and not just flesh beings. Yes, we are encased in a body of flesh while we are on earth. But we are spirits and He communicates with our spirit man, and not with our flesh.

The *Sermon on the Mount* Was Preached to the Spirit of Man

MATTHEW 5:8 "Blessed are the poor in spirit, for theirs is the Kingdom of Heaven. Blessed are those who mourn, for they shall be comforted. Blessed are the meek, for they shall inherit the earth. Blessed are those who hunger and thirst for righteousness, for they shall be satisfied. Blessed are the merciful, for they shall obtain mercy. Blessed are the pure in heart, For they shall see God. Blessed are the peacemakers, for they shall be called sons of God. Blessed are those who are persecuted for righteousness' sake, for theirs is the Kingdom of Heaven. Blessed are you when men revile you and persecute you and utter all kinds of evil against you falsely on My account; rejoice and be glad, for your reward is great in heaven, For so men persecuted the prophets who were before you."

Christ Jesus' *Sermon on the Mount*, as recorded in Matthew 5-7, sets the tone for His ministry. Preached early in His ministry, probably before all the twelve had been chosen, it is apparent that many who believed in Him were present. For, when Jesus was prepared to preach, He saw the size of the multitude that had gathered around Him, and decided to go up on the mountain. When He did, His true disciples followed Him. It is important to note that this sermon was preached to the spirit of man and not to his flesh— to all the New Covenant Generation, from that day forward. This becomes evident when Jesus begins His sermon by opening His mouth and introducing His disciples to His Spirit. What have become known as the Beatitudes, as Jesus speaks them forth He is truly declaring nine bountiful blessings upon His disciples— empowering those who came to Him on the mountain and opened their hearts as willing vessels to receive whatever Jesus could teach them. Surely those present would not reap their blessings until they received the power of the Holy Spirit after Jesus had been crucified, resurrected, and ascended, but the Holy Spirit did come to them who prayed and awaited His arrival as Jesus had promised them (Acts 1:8 & 4:8-31). And the joyous sound of each of these blessings resonates in our lives today. And we know that the blessings of the Beatitudes, and truly the entire *Sermon on the Mount*, represent a prophetic message intended for the entire New Covenant Generation. Not only is Jesus declaring blessings of the abundant life to those present when He delivered His sermon, but also to all of His disciples in every New Covenant Generation who believe in God's Word as the truth— and who apply it to their own lives and circumstances. We are His disciples on earth today; Jesus was preaching the Word of God to us.

How Do We Know the *Sermon on the Mount* Was for Man's Spirit?

Man's flesh cannot receive blessings of empowerment. Only the spirit of man is capable of understanding and receiving these blessings. Note in verse 3, the first words Jesus spoke were, *"Blessed are the poor in spirit, for theirs is the Kingdom of Heaven"* (Matthew 5:3). Our spirit man knows that we are totally dependent upon God for the forgiveness of the sins of our flesh, our daily sustenance, strength, direction, understanding, and everything else in life. When we humble ourselves before Him, and present ourselves to Him as a living sacrifice, we come unto Him stripped of any and all claims that family, land and all other things of value on earth might have on us. And God, in His mercy and love for us as His children and *City Dwellers* in Zion, will establish us as kings and priests on earth— under the royal authority of His Son Jesus; and give us the abundant life. When we realize that we are completely helpless to do anything of value on our own; and we surrender all we have back to our Father— to Whom it truly belongs, we are prepared to follow Him and our Lord Jesus. Our spirit man must control our flesh, including our mind. Our spirit man knows that we cannot outgive God. And our spirit man surely understands that the Beatitudes are our empowerment blessings.

Remember the Rich Young Ruler

Remember the account of the rich young ruler (Matthew 19:16-30). He came to Jesus, asking Him what he could do to inherit eternal life, telling Jesus that he had obeyed all the commandments. But since he thought he was already perfect, which of course he was not, Jesus told him to liquidate his assets and give the proceeds to the poor, *"and you will have treasures in heaven"* (verse 21). But he could not do this because he had great possessions, and he went away in great anguish. Surely, as Jesus told his disciples, it is difficult— almost impossible, for a rich man to enter into the Kingdom of Heaven because such a man thinks that all he owns in life belongs to him and not to God.

"Blessed Are the Pure in Heart, for They Shall See God"

John 1:18 tell us that *"No man has ever seen God; the only Son, who is in the bosom of the Father, He has made Him known"*; and I John 4:12 says, *"no man has ever seen God; if we love one another, God abides in us and His love is perfected in us."* "Is this a paradox?" we ask ourselves. It surely seems these verses contradict Matthew 5:8. No, there is no paradox here. Our spirit man is capable of understanding the meaning of all three verses, whereas our flesh is mystified. We see God in the Spirit as Jesus has made Him known to us. We surely see Him as our love for the brethren is made known to the Father; and I John 3:14 tells us that *"We know that we have passed from death to life because we love the brethren."* Our spiritual senses are at work. More than that, we know that because Jesus prayed the Father for us at the Last Supper for us to be one in Him and the Father, and they are One in us, (John 17:20-24), our spirits can go to Zion, even into the Father's throne room where we can sit down at the Father's right hand with Jesus— that where He is, we can be also; and be strengthened; and come out again, and find good pasture and the abundant life in Jerusalem. What our flesh cannot comprehend, our spirit man understands. What Jesus told the eleven at the Last Supper surely holds true for us today, *"He who has seen Me has seen the Father. How can you say, 'Show us the Father'?"* (John 14:9).

Therefore, we know that the *Sermon on the Mount* was preached to the spirit of man. Our spirit man declares things into existence just as our Father did in the beginning. Our Father earnestly desires to say to us, *"This is My Beloved son — My Beloved daughter, of whom I am well pleased* "(Matthew 3:17). To hear Him proclaim what we mean to Him, we must be in the Spirit. To do so, we need to spend quality time in the throne room with Him and our Lord Jesus.

Listening Is a Spiritual Sense When We Are in the Spirit

Listening to the voice of the Holy Spirit within us opens our spiritual ears, and helps us to know what to do in our battle with the devil. So, we listen carefully to what Jesus preaches in His *Sermon on the Mount* and to what He teaches us throughout the gospel accounts of His ministry. Knowing that Jesus has prepared a place in Zion for us and He awaits us there now urges us onward. And because of what our Lord Jesus did for us at Calvary, our gift of salvation gives us the opportunity to receive the Baptism in the Holy Spirit that purchases us a ticket to walk the highway hand-in-hand with Jesus. With Him holding our hand, we can go through all the doors of the City— even into the Father's throne room. Without the use of our spiritual senses we will never hear His voice calling us or be able to listen. The multitude who came to see and hear Jesus on the occasion of His *Sermon on the Mount* included many unbelievers— Scribes, Pharisees and curiosity seekers, because the fame of Jesus was spreading rapidly. But when He went up on the mountain, those who followed Him and wanted to be in close proximity to Him to hear every word He uttered were His true disciples; and Jesus surely opened their ears.

We Need to Always Know
What God Is Telling Us to Do

Exodus 14 relates the account of Pharaoh's pursuit of the Israelites after they had left Egyptian captivity. God told Moses that he had hardened Pharaoh's heart once again so that Pharaoh would chase after them in his own chariot and take his army with him— 600 hand-picked chariots and all the other chariots of Egypt with officers and horsemen (Exodus 14:6-9), and God told Moses to tell the people that He was allowing Pharaoh and the Egyptian army to come after them so that He would get the glory over Pharaoh— so the people of Israel and the Egyptians would know, "I Am God."

But fear set in among the people. Exodus 14:10-14 describes the dialogue between Moses and the fearful people. Whenever Pharaoh and his army drew near, the people were in great fear, saying to Moses, *"Is it because there are no graves in Egypt that you have taken us away to die in the wilderness?"* And Moses replied, *"Fear not, be still and stand fast— and see the salvation of the Lord, which he will work for you today; for the Egyptians you see today you will never see again. The Lord will fight for you, and you have only to be still."* But even Moses did not listen carefully enough to God's instructions— because when the Egyptians were almost upon them, he was still waiting for God to miraculously save them. Moses must have been pleading, "Please God, be a man of your Word and save us;" for God became provoked, commanding Moses, *"Why do you cry to me? Tell the people to go forward, lift up your rod, and stretch out your hand over the sea and divide it, that the people may go on dry land through the sea. And I will harden the hearts of the Egyptians so that they shall go in after them, and I will get the glory over Pharaoh, his chariots, and his horsemen."*

Have We Fine-tuned Our Listening Skills?

The Israelites' deliverance from Egypt is a perfect example of our need for the spiritual sense of fine-tuned listening. Remember that when God called Moses He equipped him with His rod of power and authority to use against Pharaoh. But God had to prompt Moses when to use it— and as long as He did, Moses obeyed "to the letter". In the heat of the battle, Moses forgot what he held in his own hand— the rod of power. For as the Egyptians drew nearer and nearer, all Moses knew to do was to pray fretfully, waiting on God to perform a miracle— not realizing that God had given him the rod, His power and authority to do the impossible. Moses forgot that he had the Holy Spirit with him— that he could have moved the people forward and parted the Red Sea. He needed prompting.

Empowered Believers Have a Rod and Staff

So it is with Christians today. Many brethren have not received the Baptism in the Holy Spirit, and therefore are not equipped to stand against satan. These Christians are mere babes in Christ, and lack God's power and authority— His rod and staff, to identify them and arm them for battle. Moses did not have the fine-tuned spiritual listening skill that the Holy Spirit's baptism gives us. So when the battle became a life or death issue, Moses was not able to handle it— he was only able to handle the preparation for the battle. He believed God for deliverance, but forgot that he had the power and authority in his hand to deliver the people. Moses, a servant of God, had to wait until God told him to move on— into the Red Sea, and to use his rod to roll the water back so that the Israelites could walk across on dry ground.

David Prophesied That New Covenant Believers Have the Rod and Staff

The Holy Spirit's Baptism gives us the true meaning of the very familiar Psalm 23:4. Here the psalmist David was prophesying about how spirit-filled New Covenant believers are now equipped with the weapons they need to deliver them from evil, declaring, *"Though I walk through the valley of the shadow of death, I fear no evil; for thou art with me; thy rod and thy staff, they comfort me."* Note the verse says that we walk through the valley only of the "shadow of death."

Turning to Psalm 91:1-2, we hear Moses' prayer, declaring, *He who dwells in the shelter of the Most High, who abides in the shadow of the Almighty, will say to the Lord, "My refuge and my fortress; my God, in Whom I trust."* With the empowerment of the Holy Spirit within us, we know that we have God's rod and staff— His power and authority with us always.

It's a Blessing to Know Where We Dwell and In Whose Shadow We Stand

Therefore, knowing that at Calvary our Lord Jesus defeated the power death had over us after Adam fell; and knowing where we dwell and in whose shadow we stand, we put on the whole armor of God (Ephesians 6:10-18). And we shall not fear death's shadow— as we joyously, eagerly and confidently carry our Lord's standard to identify who we are and in whose authority. We continue to carry out the commission Jesus gave us, preparing ourselves for every skirmish and every battle we must fight against the powers of evil on the earth.

Jesus Is Still in the Pasture.

John 10:9 teaches us why it is so important that we go to Zion daily. As the psalmist declares in

Psalm 84:10, *"One day in Thy courts is better than a thousand elsewhere."* Jesus tells us, *"I am the Door; if anyone enters by Me, he will be saved, and will go in and out and find pasture."* Pasture where? Jesus is talking about the need for us to return to the heavenly pasture in Zion today where the Good Shepherd awaits our arrival now. That's right. We are His sheep; and He wants us to enjoy the fullness of this life here on earth—in our Jerusalem, so we can appreciate all the more what awaits us above the threshold in the Age of Jubilee. He wants to show us how to prosper just as He did the prophet Jeremiah (Jeremiah 29:11). God thinks of us every moment; He has plans for us. And the Holy Spirit is ready to take us up to Zion. Jesus has so much to tell us, to show us. From the moment that He meets us on the highway for the redeemed (Isaiah 35); as we walk with Him through His garden, all about His Holy Mountain, through the city gates and into the courthouse square— and through the city, until we actually find ourselves in the banquet hall of the temple, it's the experience of a lifetime. We can have it each day we are here on earth. Jesus desires to take us into the throne room to meet with the Father, where we go from our strength to His strength (Psalm 84:7); and then we go out again to Jerusalem where we find pasture on earth under His protection and well within the sound of His voice (John 10:9).

We Hear Jesus Calling Us, *"Feed My Lambs"*

Before He ascended, John 21 records the occasion when Christ Jesus paid a visit to some of the disciples who had decided to "go fishing again". Although they had caught nothing, the fact that they were using a big net indicated to Jesus that they were contemplating a career move that would take them out of His ministry. This career change did not set so well with the Lord. Nonetheless, Jesus told them to fish on the other side of the boat just as He had told them where to fish when He first called them to be His disciples (Luke 5:1-11), and the disciples again caught so many fish that they could hardly bring them in. Then they recognized Jesus and came ashore to share a meal with Him.

When they had dined, Jesus asked them to make the same choice again— whether they wanted to fish for fish or fish for men. He was once again calling them to service, but they had to make their own choice. Addressing Peter directly, Jesus asked Peter if he loved Him several times, telling him to, *"Feed My lambs... Tend My sheep... Feed My sheep."* Jesus wanted Peter to know the cost of his discipleship— requiring continued commitment to His ministry— to not just say he loved Him, but to walk in his love (John 21:15-17). By placing ourselves in that scene, in Peter's shoes, we know what we are required to do. We have a free will, yes, but Jesus is charging each one of us who is His true disciple, *"Feed My lambs."*

We Bless Ourselves as We Carry Out Our Commission

We can learn much from the above passage. God will enable us to bless ourselves as we are about the business of the Kingdom. We have our instructions from Jesus with the Great Commission as recorded for us in Matthew 28:18-20, also given to His disciples before He ascended. Just like Jesus instructed Peter and the others who had "gone fishing", God does not intend for us to allow anything or anyone to take first place over Him. Jesus is the Baptizer. He intends for us to disciple His lambs and communicate the Baptism in the Holy Spirit to them all, so they too may be where He is— in Zion now, receiving their battle armor and further instructions.

We Have His Power and Authority on Earth

LUKE 10:16 **"He who hears you hears Me, and he who rejects you rejects Me, and he who rejects Me rejects Him Who sent Me."**

The pattern for our discipleship and carrying out our commission has been given to us by Jesus Himself. You will recall in Luke 9:1-6 that Jesus sent His disciples out into the towns and villages, armed with His power and authority over all demons and to cure diseases, to stay where they were received and where they were not received to leave kicking the dust off their feet; and they preached the gospel of the Kingdom of God and healed everywhere. In like manner, as Luke 10:1-2 records, Jesus appointed seventy others, sent them on ahead of Him, two by two, into every town and place where He himself was about to come, saying to them, *"The harvest is plentiful but the laborers are few; pray therefore the Lord of the harvest to send out laborers into his harvest."* Note that Jesus charged the seventy in the same manner that He charged the twelve and gave them the power and authority to heal the sick and proclaim the Word (Luke 10:9).

"I'm Going to Mount Zion
Before the Final Roll Call"

Zion won't just be a thousand times better than life on earth — nor will it be ten thousand times better — it will be immeasurably better — infinitely better. In that day we will rest from all our labors in this life. But Jesus has made it possible for us *City Dwellers* to go to Mount Zion before the final roll is called. He wants us to know the truth about what is available to us in Zion now, in this age. Remember what Jesus declared to us in John 8:31-32, *"If you continue in My Word, you are truly My disciples — and you will know the truth and the truth shall set you free."* *"Free from what?"* the Pharisees asked, not believing they were in bondage to anyone. *"Free* from the sin that enslaves you," Jesus answered. "The slave does not continue in My Father's house forever; the Son continues forever" (John 8:33-35). At the Last Supper, as recorded for us in John 14:6, Jesus declares to us, "I am the Way, and the Truth, and the Life. No one comes to the Father but by Me." Throughout His ministry, Jesus is trying to show us how we can live the abundant life here on earth— while we are sojourning. We have an inheritance, and He wants us to be able to access part of it in this life. So, again in these passages, Jesus is talking about opening wide the doors to Zion so we can receive what God wants us to have while we are still here in the flesh— divine prosperity.

What Is Our Abundant Life Multiple?

MARK 4:20 "But those that were sown upon the good soil are the ones who hear the Word and accept it and bear fruit, thirtyfold and sixtyfold and a hundredfold."

In Psalm 84:10, the psalmist was not speaking about the magnificence of life in the hereafter. No, his declaration that one day in God's courts is worth more than a thousand elsewhere is spoken about a man who knows what he is talking about. The gift of salvation, given to us unconditionally by a loving Father, entitles all believers to enter into our eternal rest when our flesh can no longer sustain us on earth. The psalmist tells us that when we dwell in Zion for just one day, our prosperity on earth is improved by at least a thousand times. Now, let's do some simple "earthly math". If one day spent with the Lord in Zion is worth 1,000 days on earth, then two days there is worth 2,000 days on earth, and so on. That's the great blessing. But there's so much more. Under the Old Covenant, Job received twice as much blessing at the end of his long ordeal of suffering after praying for his friends (Job 42:10). We can have a hundredfold blessing now.

How Much Is a Hundredfold Return?

A hundredfold return is almost incalculable because the multiple is always 100. But we know as *City Dwellers* that we can have it. Righteous Job lived under the Old Covenant and received a twofold return, a multiple of two, or twice as much after his ordeal ended than he had before his calamities started— and he was already the richest man in the East (Job 1:1-3). It's almost unimaginable how rich he would have become with the multiple of 100. We are the blessed and beloved *chosen generation.* Genesis 26:12 tells us that Isaac, the child of the promise, received a hundredfold return in one year— and Isaac also lived under the Old Covenant. We are also children of the promise God made to Father Abraham, that by his righteousness we can bless ourselves (Genesis12:3), having received the spirit of adoption into the Kingdom. And when we cry, *"Abba, Father."* it is that very Spirit of God witnessing with our spirit that we are God's children, and if children, then joint heirs with Jesus of the Kingdom of God (Romans 8:14-17; Galatians 4:5-7). God blessed Isaac with the hundredfold return in that one year as a message to us who are the New Covenant Generation. If Isaac could get that return in one year, can we not have the hundredfold return every year? Yes, we can. Jesus discusses our multitudinous return in Mark 4 in the *Parable of the Sower*.

Again in Mark 10, Jesus makes the point of the hundredfold return principle when He discusses the rich young ruler who asked Jesus what he had to do to inherit eternal life. After the rich man told Jesus that he had observed all God's commandments from his youth, Jesus told him to sell everything he owned and to give the proceeds to the poor; and to follow Him. But the rich man went away sorrowful for he had great possessions and could not relinquish his own wealth.

What do you suppose would have happened if the rich man had done as Jesus commanded? Again, his riches would have been so enormous that he could not have counted his wealth. And if he had reinvested the 100-fold return, no doubt he would have rivaled any of today's wealthiest multi-billionaires.

What Are We Willing to Surrender to God?

Jesus was making a point he wants us to learn in Mark 10:29-30, *"Truly I say unto you, there is no man who has left house, or brothers, or sisters, or father, or mother, or wife, or children, or lands, for My sake and the gospel's, but that he will receive an hundredfold now in this time, houses and brothers, and sisters, and mothers, and children, and lands, with persecutions, and in the world to come eternal life."* We really don't have a claim to anything we might "own" in this world. God really owns it all. We are stewards— caretakers. But He expects us to invest whatever He has given us for safekeeping, and use our faith to increase it, whether it is a two-fold return, twice as much; or a 30-fold, or 60-fold; or even a 100-fold return. We dare not take what God has given to us and bury it in the ground as did the unfaithful servant in Jesus' *Parable of the Talents* (Matthew 25:14-30). In the end, the servant lost the one talent he had been given, and paid dearly for his unfaithfulness.

We Are Standing on Holy Ground

EXODUS 3:5 "Take off your shoes for the place on which you are standing is holy ground."

Our way is known to God, and our foot will not slip when we are doing God's bidding here on earth. We must realize that we are spirits, continually and constantly in God's presence. When Moses was called by God out of the burning bush, God told him, *"remove your shoes from your feet because the ground on which you are standing is Holy Ground"*. Why did God require this? Because God knew that He had Moses' attention when Moses saw the burning bush and turned aside from tending his father-in-law's flock of sheep. When he did, he found himself in the presence of God; and when God called his name, *"Moses, Moses."* and Moses answered, *"Here am I"* (Exodus 3:1-6), God's very presence made the ground holy where Moses stood. Surely the prophet Isaiah knew that he was standing on holy ground when he saw the Lord sitting upon a throne, high and lifted up; saw the seraphim standing above Him, and saying to one another, *"Holy, Holy, Holy is the Lord of hosts, the whole earth is full of His glory."* Isaiah knew he was in the presence of God when God asked, *"Whom shall I send, and who will go for us?"* and he answered, *"Here am I, send me"* (Isaiah 6:1-9).

What can we learn here? If the ground was made holy for Moses and Isaiah, God can make it holy for each one of us— all *City Dwellers*, when we turn aside from going our own way to acknowledge God's presence; and hear His voice calling our name— calling us to serve Him. God needs to know if we will put His calling as the very top priority in our life's daily agenda. He knows that we are His Son's true disciples when we listen for His voice and follow Him. As our Lord Jesus declared in John 10:27, *"My sheep hear*

My voice, and I know them; and they follow Me."

God Makes Covenant with Us as He Did with the Righteous Men of Old

By His Word given to us in the beginning, God has already established us as kings and priests on earth (Revelation 5:10); and He has declared a mission for each of us, and blessed it (Matthew 5:3-16 & 28:18-20; John 14:12). All we need to do is respond to the voice of King Jesus who is calling our name just as the prophet Isaiah did (Isaiah 6:8). By the blood of Jesus shed for us at Calvary and the word of our testimony (Revelation 12:11), we can exercise our abiding faith in His Word and accept the commission Jesus offers us. Adam failed to keep faith with God and lost the blessing of dominion on earth, his under the Adamic Covenant. But grieved and disappointed as He must have been with Adam, God still called and chose men and women of great faith thereafter, with whom He would establish covenant, to witness for Him and regain the dominion on earth that Adam had lost. Thus we see God making covenant first with righteous Noah, who obeyed God and built an ark on dry land, promising Noah that He would not destroy the earth by water again (Noahic Covenant); with righteous Abraham who obeyed Him, leaving his homeland to go to a land he knew not where. This land was Israel's promised land; God promised Abraham that by His faith all the people of the earth would be able to bless themselves (Abrahamic Covenant).

God called Moses to lead His people out of captivity in Egypt; and gave Him the Law of Moses to rule the people of Israel, thus establishing the Mosaic Covenant. And God anointed David as King of Israel, establishing the Davidic lineage of kings from which Christ Jesus descended — and which gives us, his disciples on earth today, the authority of His Kingdom (Davidic Covenant). And the New Covenant in King Jesus — our Lord and Savior, under whose authority we serve as willing vessels and vassals unto Zion.

None Was Found Worthy — But We Are Worthy; Jesus Redeemed Us

Still, generation after generation, God found no one on earth worthy to dwell in Zion and establish dominion on earth. Sinful man could not be purged clean by the blood of animals; and, therefore, the gates to Zion remained shut. Before Christ Jesus came to earth, God the Father himself visited with man on earth; and He anointed whomsoever He chose to carry out specific tasks for Him on earth. But in order to enjoy daily fellowship with man, it became necessary for Him to send to earth His Own Son, the Living Word of God, who regained man's dominion over all living things that move upon the earth. Our dominion under the New Covenant surely includes our authority over evil spirits. Remember, Genesis 1:26-28 teaches us that we have power and authority over the fish of the sea, the birds of the air, and over all living things that move upon the earth. The devil and his demonic army move upon the earth. Therefore, we have dominion over such spirits. This dominion extends to lands God swore to our forefathers to give us, on which we did not labor; great and godly cities we did not build but dwell within; houses filled with good things we did not fill; and we eat the fruit from vineyards we did not plant; and draw water from cisterns we did not dig (Deuteronomy 6:10-11; Joshua 24:13). What an abundant life!

The Battle Is Against Illegal Occupants of Our Own Promised Land

JOB 1:6-7 Now there was a day when the angels presented themselves before the Lord, and satan also came among them. And God asked satan, "From whence have you come?" satan replied, "From going to and fro on the earth, and walking up and down upon it."

Demonic evil forces are moving about on the earth and must be dealt with. More to the point, they are illegally "squatting" on our God-given land and must be dispossessed. When Jesus left earth, He gave us His authority to reclaim the promised land (Matthew 28:18-20); and sent us the Holy Spirit to empower our authority over all such living things, including the power to remove them (Acts 1:8).

We Have an Infinite Advantage Over Evil

When we choose to use this power God freely gives us, we have an infinite advantage over evil— power even greater than that Adam forfeited; greater than righteous Noah (Genesis 6:9); greater yet than Father Abraham whose faith was reckoned to him as righteousness (Romans 4:3; Galatians 3:6); and which serves as an example of using spiritual principles to produce physical results on earth. Abraham's faith forms the substance of the Old Covenant.

Evil Is Deceitful— And It Moves Upon the Earth

Evil still lurks and moves about on earth today, and tries to convince us that God's Word is a lie. Adam and Eve fell from grace because the forbidden fruit satan offered them became an obsession to them and a delight to their eyes (Genesis 3:6). Somehow they became convinced by another god that the Most High God had lied to them about dying— that He knew they would become wise like Him if they ate of the fruit. Satan treacherously and deceitfully appealed to their flesh. They believed his lies, disobeyed their Creator, and lost any possibility of redemption. That day they started dying.

We cannot defeat satan in our flesh— we dare not even try. He would like nothing better than to pitch the battle against our flesh. He is spirit— just as we are, and he knows he can defeat our flesh although he lost the spiritual battle at Calvary to Christ Jesus. The devil still roars as if he were still in charge. We defeat him, spirit vs. spirit. No matter what obstacles the devil may throw at our spirit man, we win— because Jesus won the victory over him at Calvary. Because of the race of Our Lord Jesus, His Baptism of us in the Holy Spirit and by fire, His anointing to continue His ministry on earth, the gifts of the Holy Spirit, and the full armor of God, we have an arsenal of spiritual weapons to use and proclaim victory over satan.

We Were Sent to Earth from Zion

ISAIAH 6:8 And I heard the voice of the Lord saying. "Whom shall I send, and who will go for us?" Then I said, "Here I am. Send me."

We are on a mission from God— which He gave to us in Zion. Our mission was not given to us on earth. We must remember that we are spirits. Isaiah 6 relates the occasion when the prophet sees the Lord high and lifted up…and above Him stood the seraphim (verses 1-2). When we are in the Spirit, we can actually envision Isaiah in the throne room of God the Father, the King of the Universe— and we hear God ask, *"Whom shall I send, and who will go for us?"* (verse 8). And then we hear Isaiah answer, *"Here I am. Send me."* And suddenly we see what Isaiah saw, and we understand we are no longer on earth. Like the prophet Ezekiel, we have visions of God and His Holy City of Zion (Ezekiel 1:1).

Visions of the Promised Land

We see Mount Zion— Beulah Land, the land of promise, our dowry that God desires for us to enjoy in this age as His Son's bride. We envision the Holy City of Zion— the temple, the courtyards, the streets, the business of city life taking place before our very eyes, and we long to be there. Yes, Zion is a real place— our homeland, a city of greatness; and we know with an absolute certainty and assurance that only the Holy Spirit of the Father and Son can give us, that this is our home. Most of all, we know that God deeply desires for us to enjoy the Holy City of Zion in this age and in the age to come— just as Jesus told us, *"You can go in and come out, and find pasture"* (John 10:9).

We Have Been Commissioned by Christ Jesus

When we understand that Zion is His Holy City, where He birthed our spirit man— the place where our spirit man now dwells, we must have that city on earth with us. Only then can we comprehend that we have been sent to earth by God to fulfill what He declared in the beginning; and whatever His specific purpose may be for each of us, we have been appointed heralds of truth by Christ Jesus to proclaim the good news of the gospel while we walk this earth— to transform the City of Jerusalem here on earth, that is, the Jerusalem where we live and work day-to-day in our bodies of flesh, into the City God visualizes: Zion on earth (Isaiah 40:9).

We Will Prosper in This Life When
We Are in God's Perfect Will

We are our Lord's disciples. We were created in God's spiritual image and likeness to do His perfect will on earth. As God the Father and our Creator assures us in Isaiah 55:11, *"My Word will not return to me void. It will accomplish what I purposed it to do; and it will prosper the thing in which I sent it."* We are that thing— and He has declared that we will prosper in this age. We know that God gave us kingship and lordship on earth from the beginning by blessing man with dominion over all living things on the earth. Shamefully, Adam lost this authority to satan. And, yes, Jesus regained it at Calvary. But the abundant life in this age and the beautiful promises of the New Covenant, must be reenacted by each of us everyday to avoid falling into the same traps and pitfalls as did the righteous man Lot. Jesus regained man's dominion so we can carry His

message to all in the world who will receive it—
beginning in our own Jerusalem.

"Am I Ready to Be
My Lord's True Disciple?"

Asking ourselves this question requires us to
ponder the true meaning of "discipleship" in our
hearts. Are we ready to forsake all other gods—
including our own flesh? In Luke 9:23-24, Jesus
reminds us that following Him will require such
a commitment, but our failure to do so will
prevent us from enjoying life in the Spirit. We
hear Him saying to us, *"If any man would come
after Me, let him deny himself and take up his cross
daily and follow Me. For whosoever will save his life
will lose it; but whosoever will lose his life for My
sake, he will save it."* By this Word, Jesus
commanded His true disciples to follow after
Him. And when we make such a commitment,
He offers His hand to us in marriage. In John
14:12, we hear Jesus commanding whosoever
loves Him, *"If you love Me, you will do the things I
have done. Even greater things will you do because I
am going to the Father."* Had Jesus remained on
earth, He would have done these things. But
what would we be doing if He were still here?
Jesus had to leave the earth to prepare a place for
us in Zion— so we could be with Him and the
Father in this age.

At the Last Supper, Jesus told us in John 14:1-3, *"I
go to prepare a place for you that where I am you may be
also. And when I go, I will come again and will take you*

to Myself that where I am you may be also." And He had to die that we might be multiplied and carry on the work of the Kingdom, commissioning us before He ascended to do just that, saying, *"All authority in Heaven and on earth has been given to Me. Go therefore and make disciples of all nations, baptizing them in the Name of the Father, and of the Son, and of the Holy Spirit — teaching them to observe all that I have commanded you; and, lo, I am with you always, even to the close of the age"* (Matthew 28:18-20). His charge is clear. We know that He has commissioned us to service in the Kingdom of God. He will give us our individual ministerial assignments in Zion.

Are We Committed to Kingdom Work?

How many times in this life have we felt like we were wandering around with no true direction? Usually when we feel this way we also feel frustrated — "trapped" in such situations with few if any options. Surely Abraham's nephew Lot felt this way after he had chosen the wrong path of life. Yes, Lot was a righteous man, but his tragic story is one too common today. He and his family were "trapped" in evil Sodom and in the end he paid a terribly high cost for his choices. He and his two daughters barely escaped the burning city with their lives, but he lost everything else — including his wife and all his earthly goods. When we examine why God allowed such calamities to come upon a righteous man we only need to focus on one truth: God the Father gave man a free will.

4

The Story of Two Righteous Men

GENESIS 12:1-4 Now the Lord said to Abram, "Get out of your country, and from your kindred, and from your Father's house, unto a land that I will show you. And I will make of you a great nation, and make your name great; and you shall be a blessing; and I will bless them that bless you and curse those who curse you; and in you shall all the families of the earth bless themselves. So Abram departed, as the Lord had spoken unto him, and Lot (his brother's son) went with him.

Genesis 13:1-13 gives us an opportunity to analyze the startling character and spiritual differences between the spiritual man Abraham and the carnal man Lot. Note in verse 4 that Lot, his nephew, went with Abraham— although God had instructed him to leave his kindred. And, despite the fact that both men had flocks, herds and tents, strife broke out between the herdsmen of Abraham and Lot. Abraham decided that it would be better for them to divide the land and go their separate ways. So, Abraham gave Lot his choice of the land; and Lot chose for himself the rich Jordan River valley that resembled the land of Egypt.

Who Is This Man, Lot?

It's easy to identify Lot. When Lot had a choice, he chose self. His choice marked him from that moment. Moreover, in giving Lot first choice of the land, Abraham showed that he was a spiritual man, one who loved his brethren as much as himself. Lot was a righteous man, but he was also a carnal man. From that very moment, the differences between the two men would become obvious in the lifestyles they led. Lot was searching for the "easy life" that he mistakenly believed would give him all he would need in his life. We know it is that elusive something satan wants us to believe is ours. And yet, what we are looking for can't be found on the earth. God does not desire or intend for us to experience Lot's frustration and tragedy — and we won't if we can just remember who we are and why we are here on earth. Surely we don't belong here. We are citizens of Zion; God's aim is to make Jerusalem a Holy City; he is counting on us to do it. God intends for Jerusalem to be a mirror image of His Holy City of Zion.

God Gave the Promised Land to Abraham and His Offspring

GENESIS 13:14-18
The Lord said to Abram, after Lot had separated from him, "Lift up your eyes, and look from the place where you are, northward and southward, eastward and westward. For all the land you see I will give to you and to your descendants forever. I will make your descendants as the dust of the earth; so that if one can count the dust of the earth, your descendants can also be

counted. Arise, walk through the length and breadth of the land for I will give it to you."

When we begin to realize the magnitude of Genesis 13:14-18, and what these verses really mean for us, we become awe-struck. Abraham and Lot chose different paths. As we read in Genesis 13:11-13, Lot chose for himself all the Jordan River valley, and Lot journeyed east. Abraham dwelt in the land of Canaan— the promised land, while Lot dwelt among the cities of the valley and moved his tent as far as Sodom; where the men were wicked, great sinners against the Lord. Lot followed his carnal instincts, continuing to sojourn. And although Lot and his two daughters were finally delivered from Sodom because of Abraham's intercession, and before the city and all its inhabitants were destroyed by fire, righteous Lot's weak faith is not strong enough to dwell in Zion and do Kingdom work. However, Abraham's faith was so great that God chose him as the prime example of how a spiritual father who offers himself up to God as a willing vessel can cause his spiritual offspring to bless themselves. Abraham became the Father of many nations— not by using his physical senses, but rather by using his spiritual senses to accomplish great things in the physical environment of the earth. When God commanded him in verses 14-15, *"Lift up your eyes from the place where you are; and look northward, southward, eastward and westward, for all the land you see I have given to you and your descendants forever,"* he was speaking not of the limited scope of Abraham's human eyes, but of his spiritual eyes which had no limits.

We have spiritual senses. In the Spirit, we occupy and have dominion over evil and its control in our lands, cities, houses, vineyards and cisterns.

City Dwellers Are Abraham's True Heirs

When God said to Abraham in Genesis 13:16, *"I will make your descendants as the dust of the earth so that if one could count the dust of the earth, your descendants can be counted,"* He was speaking about his spiritual heirs inheriting the whole earth. This reference to the dust of the earth was not given to Abraham until Lot separated himself from Abraham.

While Lot was a righteous man, we know the life he led. And, although saved by the grace of God to live in Zion in the next age, neither Lot nor his spiritual descendants can dwell in that city in this age. But Abraham's heirs, numerous as the dust of the earth, are heirs to every square inch of the earth's surface. And although physically impossible for one man to tread upon the entire earth— in the natural, spiritually it is as possible as our vision allows. Examine the profound significance of this verse!

When believers with the faith of Abraham are as numerous as the *"dust of the earth"*, God's people can and will inherit every inch of the earth's surface. There will be no way for evil to co-exist with good. Therefore, when this day comes, will it not be the moment when evil will be cast off the earth to return to the heavenlies or wherever else God chooses? God expects us to use His Word of Power now. We are in awe when we ponder what this means for us on the earth. It makes us appreciate our citizenship in Zion all the more. It requires putting our faith to work— and stepping out and onto our own land to claim it (Joshua 1:3; Matthew 5:5; Hebrews 1:3; James 2:17).

Stepping Out to Claim the Promised Land

Now let's look closely at Genesis 13:17. When God told Abraham, *"Arise, and walk through the length and breadth of the land, for I will give it to you,"* again He was speaking spiritually, although surely Abraham did walk much of this land during his lifetime. Stepping out onto the promised land is a spiritual principle that when applied in faith will produce the desired manifestation in the physical realm. Generations later God instructed another faithful servant to do the same thing to claim the promised land. When God appointed Joshua to lead His people over the Jordan River and into the promised land, God told him that He would give him *"Every place that the sole of your foot treads upon"*; provided, however, that he meditated in the Book of the Law day and night— and was very courageous (Joshua 1:2-9). God was really telling Joshua that he was a spiritual descendant of Abraham— an heir of the promised land, but that he would be required to keep the faith as he carried out God's instructions, no matter what obstacles he would face.

We Shall Inherit the Earth— By His Grace Abiding in Us

MATTHEW 5:5 "Blessed are the meek for they shall inherit the earth."

GALATIANS 6:18 "Brethren, the grace of Our Lord Jesus Christ be with your spirit."

It takes great faith to inherit the earth. But dare we ever doubt His Word of Power which upholds all things (Hebrews 1:3). We have many blessings as His disciples that Jesus gave us in His *Sermon on the Mount*, one of which is the right to our own inheritance. Is this not His confirmation of our legitimate right as a citizen of Zion to subdue the earth, declared by Our Creator, in the beginning (Genesis 1:28)? By His proclamation in Matthew 5:5, the meek will inherit the earth, Jesus establishes our authority to claim and enter upon the promised land that He regained for us at Calvary. Jesus specifically refers to Abraham's heirs during His *Sermon on the Mount*. When He proclaims in Matthew 5:5, *"Blessed are the meek, for they shall inherit the earth,"* it means that we are enabled by the grace of Christ Jesus to use His Name to claim our promised land inheritance.

What Prevents Us from Enjoying the Blessings of Abraham?

HEBREWS 12:1-2   Let us lay aside every weight, and the sin which so easily besets us; and let us run with patience the race that is set before us, focusing our eyes on Jesus, the Pioneer and Perfecter of our faith— who for the joy that was set before Him endured the cross.

As we spend each day of this temporary life on earth encased in a body of flesh and bones, we become more accustomed to ourselves as earthly matter with weight. God gave us a body of matter so we could live on earth, but we truly come from another place where we have substance without the weight of earthly matter. And while we are here we are subject to attack by the spiritual powers of darkness from which God separated us in the beginning, but who have taken up residence on earth. And we don't want them here any more than God did.

What Prevents Us from Being Abraham's Righteous Children?

We seem to have two major obstacles facing us before we can be counted among Abraham's righteous spiritual children— heirs according to the promise: (1) poor time management, causing us to meditate too little in God's Word, thus preventing us from earnestly seeking His face; our "too busy" lifestyle causes us to focus on temporal pleasures and disappointments— thus preventing us from hearing God's voice and believing that we can receive and be empowered by the higher gifts of the Holy Spirit; and (2) our unwillingness to remove ourselves from the desires of our flesh, the day-to-day cares of this world, and the demands of the earth's physical environment— thus preventing our spirit man from dwelling in the spiritual faith realm of Zion.

The powers of evil know how to attack and establish lordship over our flesh— if we allow it to happen. But it does not need to be this way. Read Genesis 1:27 again, God gave man dominion over every living thing that moves upon the earth. This dominion surely includes our own flesh and the evil spirits that were cast out of heaven and still walk upon the earth today. As we read Job 1:7, we hear God asking satan, *"Whence have you come?"* The devil answered the Lord, *"From walking to and fro on the earth, and from walking up and down on it."* How can we walk the length and breadth of our God-given promised land if we also allow evil to walk in our footsteps?

Seeing the Promised Land in the Spirit

Again revisiting Genesis 13:14 &17. God told Abraham to lift up his eyes from the place where he was physically standing, looking in every direction— and that he had given him and his heirs this land as far as his eyes could see. What did this mean? God wanted Abraham to see the land he had promised to give him, in the spirit. Why? Because God knew Abraham could and would use his spiritual eyes to see the land of promise. When God told Abraham to walk the length and breadth of the land, God was telling him to displace the spiritual residents who still walked the earth, and to stake a spiritual claim over the land— the promised land. The devil didn't know that God had put a plan in effect in the beginning for man to regain Adam's "forfeited dominion" on earth. And the man Jesus, Himself a descendant of Abraham in the flesh, would destroy the power evil had previously exercised over mankind. Because He died for us and established the New Covenant, Abraham's faith has finally enabled all the families of the earth to bless themselves and enjoy the abundant life in the promised land on earth as *City Dwellers* in Zion.

Jesus Enabled Man to Enter the Promised Land as Victors

In the course of time, God had seen enough. Despite delivering them from bondage in Egypt,

God's people were unable to remain in the faith required for them to enter the promised land. It took a generation of living in the wilderness before Joshua successfully led God's people into the promised land — and these events are recorded in the Book of Joshua. However, the people were constantly under attack by foreign nations, spending hundreds of years in slavery and captivity. So it became necessary for God to send His only Son, Jesus, to save mankind from virtual destruction. God gave the man Jesus a mission to fulfill on earth — and a designated time for Him to fulfill it. And with His crucifixion and resurrection, He passed the torch to us.

The demonic army of spiritual outcasts and thugs now inhabiting earth must be removed. Christ Jesus gave us power and authority over all devils, and to cure diseases (Luke 9:1-2). But first we must realize that the dominion which Jesus regained for us at Calvary is spiritual in a physical world. Our physical power and might will never move the mountains the strong man throws at us. He was defeated spiritually by Jesus at Calvary; and is no match for us, spirit to spirit. God tells us in Zechariah 4:6, *"Not by power nor by might, but by My Spirit,"* saith the Lord. But we must keep our eyes focused on Jesus, the Pioneer and Perfecter of our faith (Hebrews 12:2). Our flesh might want to have everything the world has, and our pride says we can. But we cannot be trapped by the devil's wiles. We have Jesus, to whom the devil offered all the kingdoms of the world, but who chose victory, giving us the abundant life and making us one in Him (Luke 4:5-13; John 10:10).

Only *City Dwellers* Can Remove and Displace Evil from the Earth

JOHN 14:23 Jesus said to them, "If a man loves Me, he will keep My Word, and My Father will love him, and We will come and make Our home with him.

We are *City Dwellers*— God's spiritual children, spirits whom He created in His Own image and likeness— and gave dominion over all living things on the earth (Genesis 1:26-27). John 14:23 tells us how close we are to Zion. If we can envision where home is, we can get there now. Commissioned by Jesus, we have been sent to earth on a mission for the Kingdom to remove and displace evil and the evil residents of the earth. When we "wander off", we have given in to the world and the demands of our own flesh— either because we have lost our way and forgotten that we were called according to God's purpose (Romans 8:28); or because we have abandoned our first love (Revelation 2:4). Either way, our faith has faltered— we become prodigals, and we cannot return to Zion and claim our citizenship privileges unless and until we identify and correct our lifestyle. The lost son did just that in Jesus' *Parable of the Prodigal Son* (Luke 15:11-32). Once he did acknowledge the mistakes of his life, he came home repentant, to his father's great joy. What a wonderful celebration it must have been— a Year of Jubilee. The lost son had been released from captivity (Leviticus 25:10). His father came running to greet and embrace his lost son when he saw him returning home. His father forgave him, restored his position in the family, called for a banquet in his honor, dressed him in royal attire, and gave him His signet ring.

5

From Sojourners to Ambassadors

EPHESIANS 2:19 So then we are no longer strangers and sojourners, but we are fellow citizens with the saints and members of the household of God.

HEBREWS 11:8-16 By faith Abraham obeyed when God called him to go out to a place which he was to receive as an inheritance. And he went out not knowing where he was to go. By faith he sojourned in the promised land, as in a foreign land... These men and women of old died not having received what was promised — but having seen it and greeted it from afar, they acknowledged that they were strangers and exiles on earth...For people who speak this way make it clear that they were seeking their homeland. If they had been thinking of that land from which they had gone out, they would have had opportunity to return.

Where Eagles Fly, a companion book to *City Dwellers,* tells the story of a sojourner on earth who became an ambassador for Christ Jesus. His story is truly one of victory. Instead of wandering aimlessly on earth as a man of flesh — a stranger in a foreign land, he chooses to go home in the spirit, and enter into a blood covenant with His risen Lord Jesus. We can make that same choice. The book describes how the sojourner received his long sought after Baptism in the Holy Spirit — and how he found himself suddenly walking with Jesus on the highway to Zion. One day in Zion changed his life forever, and he became an ambassador for the King of kings. He allowed his spirit man to direct his life— and, in that moment, he overcame his own flesh. During His *Sermon on the Mount* (Matthew 6:24; Luke 16:13), Jesus teaches us, *"No man can serve two masters."* In the *Parable of the Sower* (Mark 4), Jesus explains this dichotomy that faces us. God desires to sow His Word into our hearts, but we cannot receive His Word and listen to the devil's lies. Because we choose God, we should expect tribulations and persecutions to come— but we must endure. We cannot choose God and satisfy the delight of our eyes, fall prey to the deceitfulness of riches, or place our desire for other things before the perfect will of God.

The sojourner realized that he could not serve God if his flesh kept getting in the way. His Baptism in the Holy Spirit opened the gates of Zion, and allowed him to go up to Zion on that very day— in that very moment, up to sweet Beulah Land in the now, and did not require him to wait until he took his last breath on earth. Immediately upon receiving the Baptism while he was kneeling at the altar in the church sanctuary, he was in the spirit, going up, and experiencing an unbelievably amazing day of celebration with Christ Jesus and the heavenly host in Zion. What a day it was. Every time he envisioned it the impressions of his experience of just one day in the Holy City became more vivid and more memorable. He found God's perfect will; he knew he could go up to his homeland.

We All Begin Life on Earth as Sojourners in a Foreign Land

Despite the glamour the world seems to dangle in front of our eyes, it's really full of wispy illusions the evil spiritual residents conjure up. We all begin our journey as strangers on Planet Earth— sojourning in a foreign land. Our frustration occurs because we have been programmed to believe that we are permanent citizens of the USA, Canada, or wherever else we call home in this life. We are not. Just as recorded for us in Hebrews 11:16, we have a city— a homeland that we can call our own; and a city where we can dwell all the days of our life on earth. Try as we might, it is impossible for us to find what we seek on earth. We must go home to find direction. As the old saying goes, "Home is where the heart is." But without studying Hebrews 11 it is impossible for us to understand the meaning of sojourning or find our way home.

We Are No Longer Sojourners— We Dwell in Zion at Jerusalem

EPHESIANS 2:19 We are no longer strangers and sojourners, but we are fellow citizens with the saints and members of the household of God.

Today we have been blessed by God to live under the New Covenant of the Blood of Christ Jesus. Because of His life on earth, crucifixion and resurrection, and the Holy Spirit Whom Jesus sent to us, we have a heavenly homeland in Zion where Jesus lives today with the Father. Therefore, history does not need to repeat itself. After Adam fell from grace, Noah, Abraham and all the other righteous men and women of faith who lived before and under the Old Covenant could not find their way home. They knew they had a homeland, but they neither knew where it was nor could they find the way to it. Why? Because their bodies could not be purged of sin. God could not forgive them because the sacrificial blood of animals was unclean and unable to atone for their sins. Hebrews 11 describes the difficult path our forefathers endured in their fruitless search for the city which has foundations, whose builder and maker is God (verse 10). They did not have Christ Jesus with them — and His blood to wash away their sins; nor did they have the ever-abiding Holy Spirit as we do. God could not forgive their sins; and although they were well-attested by their faith, they did not receive what was promised, since God had foreseen something better for us, that apart from us they should not be made perfect (verses 39-40).

Hebrews 11 records the actions of many men and women of faith. By faith, Enoch was taken up so that he should not see death, but before he was taken he was attested as having pleased God (verse 5); by faith, Noah built an ark on dry land to save mankind from the oncoming flood in obedience to God (verse 7); by faith, Abraham obeyed God when he was told to go to the place of his inheritance he knew not where, and sojourned in the promised land (verses 8-9) — and, by his faith, Abraham was obedient to God and willing to sacrifice his own son Isaac, the child of the promise through whom God had told him that all the families on earth would bless themselves, believing that God would raise him up again even if he were dead (verses 17-19); by faith, Moses kept the Passover to save the first-born of Israel, and led the people of Israel out of Egypt and across the Red Sea on dry land (verses 28-29); by faith, with Joshua leading them, the walls of Jericho fell down after the people had encircled the city seven times (verse 30).

Their Faith Alone Was Not Enough to Find the City

Despite their valiant efforts to find the city they knew was their homeland, and through their faith caused them to subdue kingdoms, work their righteousness, obtain promises, stop the mouths of lions, quench the violence of fire, escape the edge of the sword, be made strong out of weakness and courageous in battle, turn to flight the armies of aliens, and endure terrible hardships, beatings, and stonings— even to the point of sure death, they were prevented from going home (Hebrews 11:32-38).

His Blood Purged Us of All Unrighteousness

We are a New Covenant Generation— in a relationship with Christ Jesus, whose blood purged us of all unrighteousness and made us worthy to return to Zion and dwell there— even while we sojourned on earth. We have God's Word that we have been delivered from such situations and circumstances. Christ Jesus instructs us in Matthew 10:22, *"All nations will hate you because you are My followers, but you who patiently endure to the end will be delivered from them all."* And Jesus reminds us again of His presence in Matthew 28:20, when He commissions us as His ambassadors to continue His work just before His ascension, that yes, times will be tough on occasion, but, *"I am with you always, even to the close of the age."*

Our Life in Zion Begins When We Decide to Stop Sojourning

Jesus carefully instructs us in Matthew 6:24 that no man can serve two masters. When we live each day yielding to the demands of our flesh, we cannot serve God. We may suppose we can. But what we think, speak and act everyday as carnal men lacks all spiritual sense. Doubt sets in when our faith fails to bring us God's blessings, and we become doubleminded. Are we believers? Yes. Saved for eternity? Yes, by the grace of God. But James 1:6-8 tells us that our carnal ways weary us as we attempt in vain to juggle our conflicting values, to the point that we become unstable in all of our ways; and in such a state of mind, we should never suppose that we can receive anything we ask of God. And receiving no blessings from God spells defeat and unanswered prayer for salvation only Christians. But as the process of becoming a New Covenant man continues to foster our maturity, we enjoy more rights and privileges of citizenship in Zion. We find ourselves increasingly meditating in God's Word and our hunger and thirst for righteousness takes over our very being. As we seek God's face and begin to pray the Father (John 14:16) as Jesus did in intercession for our Christian brethren on the very night He was betrayed, we begin to consciously put on the full armor of God. We understand and appreciate the importance of using the Name of Jesus to get prayers answered and establish our God-given authority on earth. And when we experience our Lord Jesus as He baptizes us in the Holy Spirit and completes our baptism by fire, we see our previous defeats turning into victory. Awestruck, we can only drop to our knees in His presence as our hearts absorb the magnanimous love of God the Father, and the grace our Lord Jesus has shown us throughout our maturation— and we bask in the abiding fellowship of the Holy Spirit in us and our brethren (II Corinthians 13:14)— as we experience the joy of the Lord and His strength as one body in Christ.

Victory Is Ours When We Are
Willing to Die to Self

From the moment we land on earth, all of us begin searching for meaning in our life. John 10 and Mark 10 tell us that Jesus came to earth so we can have the abundant life now in this age— and eternal life in heaven. So when we decide that we are unwilling to wait until we take our last breath on earth before experiencing the victory Jesus promises, and open our hearts to the unction and movement of the Holy Spirit, our citizenship in Zion begins— again. That is what is required for us to receive the power and authority of King Jesus on earth. And once we do, Jesus can use us to accept and complete whatever God intends and has declared for us to do. We remain defeated until we take stock of ourselves and decide we are going God's way. It takes a while, but once we get our priorities straight, God honors our decision— and our commission begins.

The Water Baptism Is Physical
Evidence of Righteousness

Sojourners live in defeat. Despite being baptized with water, it does not give sojourners the power and authority to work for the Kingdom. Once the sojourner wants more than that, the Holy Spirit has something we need— a powerful baptism. Therefore, the Baptism in the Holy Spirit must be distinguished from the water baptism. Not to discount the water baptism because of our faith in the water itself, but the water baptism is an outward sign that we have repented of our sins, accepted Christ Jesus as our Lord and Savior by profession of our faith, and God the Father has given us the gift of eternal salvation. However, just as our water baptism is the same baptism that John the Baptist gave Christ Jesus in the River Jordan, Baptism in the Holy Spirit is also the same baptism Jesus received from God the Father on that very occasion. It is the Baptism of power that Jesus desires us to have and use today. He is the Baptizer.

The Anointing Is Not Available to Believers Who Continue Sojourning

Matthew 3:16-17 records how Jesus received the power of the anointing, Jesus went up immediately from the water, saw the Holy Spirit descending upon Him like a dove and alighting on Him, and heard His Father's voice saying, *"This is My Beloved Son with Whom I am well pleased"*. Nowhere in the Bible is it recorded that anyone present at the time of Jesus' baptism saw or heard anything to indicate that Jesus had received another Baptism. The Baptism in the Holy Spirit cannot be seen, heard, or experienced by the world. Therefore, the world constantly rejects the very mention of this kind of baptism. They cannot and will not understand it. And many church-going believers have trouble accepting it— believing just as they have been taught, that all of the higher gifts of the Holy Spirit Paul identifies in I Corinthians 12 passed away with the end of the "Apostolic Age". Hence, they continue sojourning— appreciating their salvation, but powerless to go further into their own promised land on earth that God has declared is theirs. Like ten of the twelve spies who reconnoitered the Land of Promise centuries ago, and gave a bad report (Numbers 13:25-33), many of today's Christians simply lack the faith or the armament to battle and remove the enemy from the land God intended to give them.

What Do Charismatic Christians Believe?

Charismatic Christians believe that the "Apostolic Age" is synonymous with the "New Covenant Age"— and that we who have received the Baptism in the Holy Spirit have been empowered by it, and continue to live and prosper in this age today, with prophets among us, making the abundant life available to us. Believers of this persuasion surely understand that the power of the Holy Spirit's anointing is necessary to enter into and take back our promised land that the devil occupies and has been walking upon.

Jesus Was Also a Sojourner on Earth —
Blazing the Trail for Us

When we think of "sojourning" we usually think of Abraham first— and many other Old Testament heroes— Sarah, Isaac, Jacob, Joseph, Moses, Joshua, David, Samuel and the prophets. Hebrews 11 tells their story, and their lives are a testimony to their faith. We began studying about them as children— remembering so well their stories as told in the *Child's Story Bible*; and we sing of them often today in the old hymn, *Faith of Our Fathers*. But though they all exercised their faith as God gave them the light to see, they didn't have the Living Word of God in Christ Jesus to guide them. Therefore, they were unsuccessful in finding their heavenly home because they lacked the cleansing power of His blood to make them acceptable to God the Father in Zion.

Hebrews 12:2 tells us that we need to look to another who "sojourned" on earth until His Own Baptism in the Holy Spirit and the beginning of His ministry— none other than Christ Jesus. He also walked the earth— during the last days of the Old Covenant. Remember, the New Covenant was not written until Calvary when Jesus established it with His Own blood. Matthew 27:50-53 records what happened immediately after Jesus yielded up His Spirit, ending the Old Covenant. Only then was the curtain in the temple torn in two— only then was the veil lifted to reveal the truth, show us the way home, and give us access to the Holy of Holies. Only then were the tombs of those who had died in captivity opened. For clear direction to our homeland— we must fix our eyes on Christ Jesus, the Pioneer and Perfecter of our faith (Hebrews 12:2). And He wants to show us the Way.

"Sojourner, I Am the Way to Zion— Fix Your Eyes on Me"

While we are sojourning we begin to realize that Christ Jesus is speaking to our spirit man. In His grace toward us, Jesus knows firsthand how tough the battle becomes— almost too much to endure. But because he pioneered the way for us, casting aside all roadblocks and defeating the strong man at Calvary, He has made us the victors. Even now Jesus realizes that each day our transformation from a defeated and carnal minded old man to a victorious new man is subject to attack from demonic forces trying to keep us from becoming a citizen of Zion. So we must constantly fix our eyes on Jesus to maintain our focus (Hebrews 12:2). Jesus wants to show all of us on earth today how to stop "sojourning" and start serving God. At the Last Supper and before His arrest, John 14:6 records for us a portion of what Jesus said to the eleven, *"I am the Way to Zion; I am the Truth, so believe Me when I say that I go to prepare a place for you now so that you may be with Me where I am; and I am the victorious life you can have in eternity and on earth today if you will dwell with Me and My Father now."* Jesus reminds us that on that same night He prayed the Father for us to have the power of the Holy Spirit (John 16:14); and that His message of hope would apply to us on earth today and to all His disciples in this age, saying, *"I do not pray for these only, but also for those who believe in Me through their word"* (John 17:20), He surely meant us. He wants to share all He has with us— His power, authority, victory over death, and glory.

Our Best Friend Is Waiting
for Us in Zion Today

MATTHEW 28:20   "I am with you always — even to the end of the Age."

A man I respected until the day he passed away once told me, "You can count your true friends in this life on one hand— maybe on one or two fingers." Probably very true. But as we sojourn in this foreign land we know with absolute certainty that our very best friend is in Zion, He promises to abide with us always— and is now awaiting our arrival with great joy.

A God-inspired hymn, *What a Friend We Have in Jesus,* tells us much about our mutual friendship with our Creator. God calls us "friend". John 15:13-17 records the occasion at the Last Supper when we hear Jesus telling the eleven and all of us that we are His friends before He goes to the cross, *"Greater love has no man than this, that a man lay down his life for his friends. You are my friends if you do what I command you. No longer do I call you servants, for a servant does not know what the master is doing; but I call you friends, for all that I have heard from My Father I have made known to you. You did not choose Me, but I chose you that you should go and bear fruit; and that your fruit should abide. And that whatever you ask the Father in My Name He will give it to you. This I command you — love one another."*

Praise God for Jesus, the Blessed Assurance of our inheritance of the Kingdom. With such a great promise by our Savior, we know that Jesus is the very Man who loved us, His friends, so much that He laid down His life for us and wants us with Him in Zion today (John 15:13 & 17:24). The time to "mount up" and "go up" to Zion is today.

Tired of Walking in the Flesh?
Spend More Time at Home.

EPHESIANS 2:19 We are no longer sojourners, but fellow citizens with the saints and household of God.

God created all mankind in the image and likeness of Himself and His Son; predestined all of us to serve, but called those of us whom He needed at His time certain to carry on the work of the Kingdom that He had chosen for each of us to do (Romans 8:29-30). It's hard to imagine that we were created in God's image and likeness. But we were; and since God is Spirit, we must remember that He created us in His spiritual image and likeness. Yet, we spend the majority of our time in this lifetime walking in the flesh as a sojourner on earth. The question for all of us to ask ourselves is this, How much time does my spirit man dwell in Zion? Only in Zion can our spiritual eyes and ears be opened so that we can understand the importance of the anointing made available to us as a child of God— one whom God the Father has consecrated as a king and lord to do His bidding on earth. Indeed, from the moment we know that we have received the Baptism in the Holy Spirit, we also know that everything has changed— that we have received the right and exercised the privilege of citizenship in Zion. We know that we are a new creation in Christ Jesus, that the old man we once were has gone and the new, redeemed man has come (II Corinthians 5:17).

Sojourning in the Flesh— or Dwelling in the Spirit

All of us are sojourning in the flesh on foreign soil. We don't belong here on earth. We are strangers here, but we are also on a mission— we are spirits, and our homeland is Mount Zion. Hebrews 11 relates to us the story of our Old

Covenant heroes who sojourned on earth just as we are doing today, but unlike and apart from us they could not be transformed from sojourners to ambassadors: By faith Abraham sojourned in the land of promise...looking forward to the city which has foundations, whose builder and maker is God. And though all the men and women of the Old Covenant believed in faith that they would find their homeland, they died without receiving this promise— because God had foreseen something better for us, that apart from us they should not find what they sought or be made perfect (Hebrews 11:8-40).

Old Covenant People Were Forced to Continue Sojourning

There was no savior for Old Covenant people— which meant they had to just keep right on sojourning and were prevented from ever entering their rest. They had no way to get to Zion— no matter how obedient they were to God's Word. But Christ Jesus made it possible at Calvary for all these heroes to be made perfect in Him. At the Last Supper and before his arrest, Jesus prayed the Father for all of us that through our faith in His Word, we all may become perfectly one; He glorified us by giving us His glory and making us all one Chosen Generation in Him (John 17:20-23). To seal this covenant with us—His disciples who walk the earth in the flesh today, Christ Jesus prayed in John 17:24, *"I desire that they also may be with Me where I am, to behold My glory which Thou hast given Me in Thy love for Me before the foundation of the world."* What a revelation. Jesus does not pray this to apply only in the next age— the Age of Jubilee. He wants us with Him now— in this New Covenant Age.

The Baptism by Fire Tests Our Faith and Teaches Us Perseverance

MATTHEW 3:11 "I baptize you with water for repentance, but He Who comes after me is mightier than I, Whose sandals I am not worthy to carry; He will baptize you with the Holy Spirit and with fire."

It is significant that immediately after Jesus was baptized in the Holy Spirit, Matthew 4:1 records that the Holy Spirit led Jesus into the wilderness to be tempted by the devil. Jesus gives us the Lord's Prayer in Matthew 6 during His *Sermon on the Mount,* in which verse 16 asks us to pray the Father to *"lead us not into temptation, but deliver us from evil."* So we know that Jesus must have received something of immeasurably great value after He went up immediately from the water that would prepare Him for the ordeal to come, 40 days and nights in the wilderness; which equipped Him with the strength afterwards when Jesus was at His weakest to resist the devil's temptations.

The Father Baptized Jesus with the Holy Spirit and with Fire

His 40-day ordeal in the wilderness marked the rude beginning of our Lord's Own baptism by fire. Jesus would be required to endure three years of terrible persecution by the religious authorities of His Own people— continuing until the very moment in the Garden of Gethsemane when He realized that His time had come. Realizing, too, that His disciples were not interceding for Him as He hoped they might, but rather sleeping instead of praying as He had taught them to do, we hear our Lord waking His disciples after He had prayed yet a third time, saying, *"Are you still sleeping and taking your rest? Behold, the hour is at hand that the Son of Man is betrayed into the hands of sinners. Rise, let us be going; see, My betrayer is at hand"* (Matthew 26:45-46). The message for us is clear: Jesus expects us to be vigilant in our prayer life, persevering against evil, and showing our love for our brethren. *We know that we have passed from death to life because we love the brethren* (I John 3:14).

Jesus Taught Us That Service Is a Prerequisite of Leadership

MARK 10:43-45 "Whosoever would be great among you must be your servant...For the Son of man also came not to be served, but to serve, and to give His life for many."

It is impossible for us to comprehend the love of God as manifested in Christ Jesus. It is unimaginable that even our best friend— to say nothing of the very nature of His royalty as King of kings, would willingly give up His Own Life for you and me, sinners that we are. Yet, Jesus did just that— and His final intercession for us with the Father while He was dying on a man-made cross where we should have been, was *"Father, forgive them, for they know not what they do"* (Luke 23:34)— thus fulfilling Isaiah's centuries old prophecy, *He made intercession for the transgressors* (Isaiah 53:12).

We Are Not Merely Sojourners— We Are Called to Serve and Lead

Jesus considered service to the lost of Israel to be His calling. His final act as a sojourner on earth was to ask the Father to forgive us. Anyone who desires to lead the brethren must first serve the brethren. This commandment requires learning how to be humble. When His disciples began to argue among themselves about which of them was the greatest in the Kingdom, Jesus chastised them for their arrogance in Mark 10:43-45.

God's Word records the exact moment Jesus awakened His sleeping disciples for yet a third time while He had been praying for all of us on the night He was betrayed. We hear Him declaring, *"The hour is at hand, and the Son of man is betrayed into the hands of sinners"* (Matthew 26:45). Jesus knew that His baptism by fire was over at that very moment. He knew that His time had come for offering Himself up as a "living sacrifice"; and, that no matter what He would be required to bear, Jesus was ready to be about completing the task. His baptism by fire, beginning in the wilderness after He was baptized in the Holy Spirit, had prepared Him for what was to be the most horrific and tortuous experience ever suffered by man. A final proof of Jesus' readiness for what lay ahead for Him came just a moment later when the high priest's slaves came to arrest Him: Peter drew his sword, and cut off the ear of one of the high priest's cadre of slaves who had come to arrest Jesus. Jesus immediately chastised Peter, and, healing the slave's ear, commanded him, saying, *"Put your sword away; for all who take the sword to protect themselves will perish by the sword. Do you not think that I can appeal to My Father, and He will at once send Me twelve legions of angels. But how then should the scriptures be fulfilled, that it must be so?"* (Matthew 26:51-53; Luke 22:50-51).

The Prophet Jeremiah
Was Baptized With Fire

All of us must be baptized with fire. We must be exposed to the enemy's fire before we can be assured that we can stand. One such tactic satan uses is frustration— he knows how to get to our flesh. So it was with Jeremiah who prophesied during the final days of the Kingdom of Judah when the kingdom was in severe decline. He witnessed how his people turned away from God to other gods (Jeremiah 11:10). God had seen enough and told Jeremiah that He would bring evil upon Judah from which they shall not be able to escape (verse 11:11). Jeremiah prophesied about the oncoming evil so that the people would turn back to God; and soon found himself targeted by evil men scheming to kill him. Jeremiah complained bitterly to God, who answered him in Jeremiah 12:5-6. And God's answer is one we all need to heed: *"If you have raced with men on foot, and they have wearied you, how will you compete with horses? And if in a safe land you fall down, how will you do in the jungle of the Jordan? For even your brothers and the house of your father, even they have dealt treacherously with you; they are in full cry after you. Believe them not even though they speak fair words to you."* God was preparing Jeremiah for the adversity and destruction to come by Nebuchadnezzar and the Babylonian army who would destroy Jerusalem, lay waste the land, and take most of the people captive. Like the counsel God gave Jeremiah, God tries to prepare us in advance for disappointment and discouragement. Our baptism by fire should enable us to draw strength from Zion so that we can triumph over an all-out enemy assault.

Our High Priest Jesus Is the Baptizer

MATTHEW 3:11-17 "I baptize you with water for repentance, but He Who is coming after me is mightier than I, whose sandals I am not worthy to carry. For He will baptize you with the Holy Spirit and with fire."

John the Baptist was the last of the Old Covenant Levitical priests. He baptized the people with water for the repentance of sins, but, in his own words, we hear John telling the people in Matthew 3 that Jesus was coming— One Who was mightier than he, Who would baptize them with the Holy Spirit and with fire. A priest can only pass on to the person he is baptizing what he has within him to give. Thus, when God the Father baptized Jesus, anointing Him with the power of the Holy Spirit that John the Baptist, a Levitical priest, did not have to give, the Father established the pattern for how Jesus would baptize all who seek after it— by anointing believers with power; and by allowing His disciples to communicate this baptism by the laying on of hands (Acts 19:4-6). Such a baptism causes the power from Zion to alight upon and empower believers.

Matthew 4:1 tells us that after His baptism by the Father, Jesus was led into temptation by the Holy Spirit. No, this does not contradict the Lord's Prayer that Jesus gave us (Matthew 6:13). But the fact that Jesus was so led by the Holy Spirit shows us that without the anointing, God does not lead even the most eager believers, who have not been anointed likewise, into situations to be tempted by the devil. The New Covenant written with the blood of Jesus would not be in force until Calvary; and the Baptism in the Holy Spirit would not be available to the early church until the Day of Pentecost. On that day in Jerusalem 120 believers, all of one accord and in prayer, were gathered together in Jerusalem (Acts 1:12-14). When the Holy Spirit Whom Jesus promised them in John 14:15-17 and Acts 1:5-8 came upon them, suddenly a sound came from heaven like the rush of a mighty wind, and it filled all the house where they were sitting; and there appeared to them tongues as of fire, distributed and resting on each one of them. And they were all filled with the Holy Spirit and began speaking in other tongues as the Spirit gave them utterance (Acts 2:2-4). Nothing like this had ever occurred before.

God Changed the Priesthood

GENESIS 1:26-27   Then God said, "Let us make man in Our image, after Our likeness; and let them have dominion over all the earth..." So God created man in His image and likeness male and female He created them.

A big question is answered with this baptism. Why did God the Father change the priesthood and make such a powerful outpouring possible (Psalm 110:4)? We forget so easily that we are spirits, created in the image and likeness of God the Father and the Son. We would do well to memorize Genesis 1:26-27. It is the Father Himself who declared in the beginning that man would be like Him and His Son, thus giving man the power of the Holy Spirit so that we may truly be a creative force in the earth. When Adam and Eve allowed satan to become their god (Genesis 3:1-7), man's image and likeness changed— becoming like that of evil, and their God-given domination was lost for centuries.

Our God Is a Covenant God

From the very beginning, God entered into covenant with the first man Adam, giving Him dominion over the entire earth— and the host thereof. Genesis 1:26-30 records the magnitude of the dominion that God gave Adam— total authority over the fish of the sea, the birds of the air, and over every living thing that moves upon the face of the earth. Made in His own image and that of His Son, and after their likeness, God delegated His dominion on earth to Adam, gave him a wife, and commanded them, *"be fruitful and multiply, and subdue the earth"*. Adam and Eve enjoyed God's assurance of eternal life— and He gave them a perpetual food supply, placing them in the Garden of Eden to till and keep it (Genesis 2:15).

To keep his part of the covenant, Adam was only expected to remain loyal and obedient to his Creator. Therefore, God commanded them to eat of all the trees in the garden except one— the Tree of the Knowledge of Good and Evil. And He told them, *"If you eat of this forbidden tree, you will die"* (Genesis 2:16-17). But they did, and they lost their dominion to the fallen angel of evil, Lucifer, known as satan.

Our God is a covenant God. John 3:16 describes our covenant with Him today. God gave us Christ Jesus— and whosoever receives and believes that He is Lord will inherit eternal life. Before Jesus came to earth, God entered into covenant with certain men and women of the Old Testament— Adam, Noah, Abraham, Jacob, Moses, and David were anointed by God for service that affected generations. And He anointed Joshua, Gideon, Solomon, and Mary, Jesus' mother, for special assignments. God entered into covenant relationships with His people to ensure that His declared Word would not return to Him void— that it would accomplish what He purposed it to do, and prosper the thing in which it was sent (Isaiah 55:11). God needed spiritual men He could trust to carry out His divine will on earth.

Throughout the Bible we see Him making covenant with people He chose. In this book, we group together Adam's Generations and the generations of the Pre-Noahic Age (before the flood); the generations of the Noahic Covenant, Abrahamic Covenant, Mosaic Covenant, and the Davidic Covenant. We refer to all generations before Jesus came as the Old Covenant Age.

During all of these generations, no man was found worthy to receive the restoration of man's dominion on earth. We know that God anointed a select few of His people for specific purposes— yet, none were worthy to reenter Zion, despite the altars and sacrifices made by all the Godly men and women of old to get right with God. Surely, however, there were signs and wonders God performed during this age to indicate what He intended to do for the special people He chose for Himself among all the peoples of the earth. Enoch walked with God and was taken up (Genesis 5:24); righteous Noah was blameless in his generation and walked with God (Genesis 6:9); righteous Abraham's great faith and obedience to God's Word caused his descendants to bless themselves, and to become as numerous as the stars in the heavens (Genesis 15:5); Jacob inherited Abraham's Covenant promises, through his 12 sons; God gave him power over men on earth, and renamed him, "Israel" (Genesis 28:14); Moses obeyed God, led His people out of Egypt, and recorded the Mosaic Law God gave him (Exodus 4:20; 12:31-42; 20:1-17);

David was anointed by God to be King of Israel, and established the method by which God determines who shall be anointed as kings and priests today (I Samuel 16:7-13); and all the other mighty men and women of the Bible— including the kings and prophets, served God well before the New Covenant was established.

God Knew The Way to
Get Man Back to Zion

Yet, none— no, not one, was found worthy to reenter Zion. Try as they might, the blood of animals they sacrificed to God for the forgiveness of their sins could not purify the heart of man, purge him free of sin, and make him again acceptable to God. But God knew there was a way; and, although it would be unspeakably tortuous for His Son and Himself, God sent the Perfect Lamb in the form of Jesus to the earth and gave him a body of flesh, so that we might receive the gift of salvation. And, without this assurance, mankind would continue to sojourn on earth without a purpose. We know that we are here on this earth to carry out God's purpose.

The New Covenant Redeemed Us
from the Curse of the Law

GALATIANS 3:13-14 Christ redeemed us from the curse of the Law, having become a curse for us. For it is written, "Cursed be everyone who hangs on a tree," that in Christ Jesus the blessing of Abraham might come upon the Gentiles— that we might receive the promise of the Holy Spirit through faith.

Everything changed when God the Father baptized Christ Jesus at the River Jordan. Because the Father was so well pleased with Jesus, His Beloved Son, He had found the way for fallen man to be restored to the image and likeness of His Son; and behold the glory that Jesus had enjoyed with the Father before the foundation of the world (John 17:24). But Jesus had to die for us to receive this restoration. After His crucifixion and resurrection, but before His ascension, Jesus told His disciples in Acts 1:8, *"You shall receive power from on high when the Holy Spirit comes upon you — that you may be My witnesses in Jerusalem, all of Judea and Samaria, and to the end of the earth."* With this instruction, He was confirming what He had promised His disciples at the Last Supper (John 14:23) — that He and His Father would come and dwell in those who loved Him and believed His Word. His assurance in Acts 1:8 also gave His disciples His power to exercise the authority He had given to them when He commissioned them as His ambassadors on earth (Matthew 28:18-20).

Jesus Asked the Father for Us to Be One with Them

JOHN 17:20-24 "I do not pray for these only, but also for those who believe in Me through their word of testimony, that they may be one; even as Thou, Father, art in Me, and I in Thee, that they also may be in Us — so that the world may believe that Thou has sent Me. The glory which Thou has given Me, I have given to them, that they may be one even as We are One, I in them and Thou in Me, that they may become perfectly one that the world may know that Thou has sent Me, and has loved them even as Thou has loved Me. Father, I desire that they also may be with Me where I am — to behold My

glory which Thou has given Me in Thy love for Me before the foundation of the world."

As a New Covenant man, when we are in the image of God and after His likeness, the dominion He bestowed upon us in the beginning is available to us in Zion. We have this miraculous gift because Christ Jesus prayed the Father that we might be one in Him and the Father— that our image and likeness to God might be restored. Once we are restored we can be in Zion again— to behold the glory of our Lord Jesus.

Note that Jesus prayed in John 17:23 that we might become perfectly one. This is what the Baptism of Fire is all about. Jesus is the Baptizer and He intends for us to behold some of His glory in Zion as we whom He baptizes in the Holy Spirit are in the process of becoming the perfect new man.

Therefore, as we go through the fire, He asks the Father to allow us to be with Him— in Zion where He is, where we receive strength and counsel to help us carry out the commission He has given to each of us. Jesus is talking about us being with Him in the throne room of the Father— to communicate freely with both Him and the Father, to walk the highway to Zion, and spend some time with Him in the Garden of Eden.

May the Grace of Our Lord
Be with Us in the Fire

II CORINTHIANS 12:9 "My grace is sufficient for you, for My power is made perfect in your weakness."

When we invite our Baptizer, Christ Jesus, to baptize us in the Holy Spirit, just as His Father baptized him; and to baptize us with fire to burn our sticky chaff away, we are ready to begin honoring our commission as His ambassador for the Kingdom of God. As we are being reconciled to the image and likeness of God the Father and the Son, two self-made mountains that hinder us from enjoying fellowship with them both in Zion are self-pity and selfish pride. With so much on the line, dare we let these weaknesses of our flesh keep us from going to Zion and enjoying our rights and privileges of citizenship in our homeland.

Are We Overcomers?

Ask yourself if you are an overcomer. No matter that we have repented, confess our sins daily and go to church every Sunday, love God and our brethren, have and use great faith to receive what we hope for, believe in the power of the Word, try to keep God's commandments, believe our armor will defend us, pray in the Spirit always— with a prayer language only known to God, the weaknesses of self-pity and selfish pride must be conquered by our new man in Christ. Study

104

Revelation 12:11. This passage of scripture tells us that we are overcomers— that we have conquered evil by the blood of the Lamb and the word of our testimony. Look in the mirror. Sometimes the one part of our chaff that prevents us from enjoying time in Zion with Jesus and the Father is right in front of our eyes. Mark 4:12 tells us why— we see but don't perceive.

Our Lord's Grace Is the Part of Armor That Helps Us to Conquer Self

II Corinthians 12:7-10 tells us that the Apostle Paul had a problem of the flesh. It may have been a physical thorn; or it could have been some kind of insecurity on his part— especially since his reputation as Saul of Tarsus was that of a murderer. Perhaps it was some other impediment of the soul. We don't know what it was, except that it was a thorn; and, despite him asking God to remove it on three occasions, the Lord told him, *"My grace is sufficient for you, for My power is made perfect in weakness"* (II Corinthians 12:9). When the Apostle discusses this problem, he had just completed relating to the Corinthians occasions about himself and the many abuses he had suffered, detailing his countless beatings where he experienced great pain and suffering, including a stoning and shipwreck. And in the following chapter (II Corinthians 12:1-6), he boasts of his own visions and revelations he had of the Lord, describing a true and lasting experience of how a man was caught up into Paradise. In verse 7, he tells of how he felt that God had given him a thorn to prevent him from boasting too much about his "abundance of revelations".

The key for us to remember is the grace of our Lord Jesus. We need His grace everyday — especially as we battle self. Paul had a similar battle. Jesus knows exactly what we are going through in our walk of faith; and He wants His grace to be sufficient for us to overcome self. He will help us to take away our self-pity which even Paul displays occasionally in His letters; and our selfish pride, whether of the soul — or of the spirit, which seems to be Paul's concern as he catches himself boasting of his spiritual encounters. Remember, Jesus baptized us with fire just as the Father had baptized Him, so He knows the cost of our perseverance — and wants to help us carry the load. Even on the very night Jesus was betrayed, He needed His Father's help, as He was praying, *"Father, remove this cup from Me if You are willing"* (Luke 22:42); and the Father sent an angel from heaven to strengthen Him (verse 43).

Notice here that God the Father did not remove the cup, but sent Jesus an angel to strengthen Him. We can count on Jesus for similar relief.

God Commanded Man to Have Dominion

GENESIS 1:27-28   So God created man in His Own image, in the image of God He created Him, male and female He created them. And God blessed them; and God said to them, "Be fruitful and multiply, and fill the earth and subdue it; and have dominion over the fish of the sea, and over the birds of the air, and over every living thing that moves on the earth."

In the beginning, God created man in His Own image and after His likeness; and God gave man dominion over the (1) fish of the sea; (2) birds of the air; and (3) all living things that moved upon the earth. At the same time God also commanded man to be fruitful and multiply; and subdue the earth (Genesis 1:26-28).   With these two commands, God established man as His multiple kings on earth— rulers on earth that He needed. When God cast traitor Lucifer and His turncoat angels out of heaven, and below the threshold— one third of the angelic host, He knew they would occupy the earth (Revelation 8:7-12). And God knew it would take spiritual kings to rid the earth of such a powerful force of evil. Therefore, God told man, *"Be fruitful and multiply, and subdue the earth*— and He later told Abraham, *"your descendants will be more populous than all the stars in heaven"* (Genesis 15:5). God desired for His kings to be a greater force than all of the fallen angels on earth— and to exercise dominion over these evil spirits and subdue them.

God's Purpose for Man on Earth

EZEKIEL 28:17 "Your heart was proud because of your beauty; you corrupted your wisdom for the sake of your splendor. I cast you to the ground; I exposed you before kings."

Ezekiel 28:13-19 helps us to understand how God is revealing His true purpose for man— to take back the earth for Him. We hear God proclaim that Lucifer's perverted criminal mind— his treachery and deceitfulness, would cause him to come to a dreadful end, *"I cast you as a profane thing from the mountain of God...I cast you to the ground and exposed you before kings...I brought forth fire from the midst of you, and it consumed you; and I turned you to ashes upon the earth in the sight of all who saw you. All who know you among the peoples are appalled at you; you have come to a dreadful end and shall be no more forever"*.

We are the kings God refers to in verse 17. God never intended for man to exercise dominion on earth without first going to Zion. In the beginning, He created the heavens and the earth, and the hosts thereof, by declaring these things into existence with the words of His mouth— and He saw these things appear on earth as good (Genesis 1:31). It is important to note that God first saw them appear in His Spirit. He envisioned them when they were not. Faith in His Own Word caused them to be manifested on earth.

Our Relationship to God Is
Spirit to Spirit

God gave dominion on earth to the spirit man Adam— God's Spirit to man's spirit. Man's dominion over things on earth is spiritual dominion. However, once they appear on earth, we have authority in the earth over all these things. Until they actually appear on earth, such things remain in Zion; or are in transit from Zion to Earth; or are being held in captivity here on earth. These last two points need emphasis. As Galatians 5:22-24 teaches us, *"The fruit of the Spirit is love, joy, peace, patience, faithfulness, gentleness, and self-control; and whosoever belongs to Christ Jesus has crucified the flesh with its passions and desires."* Among all works of the flesh, selfishness (Galatians 5:20) especially stands out as a work of our flesh which demands immediate satisfaction; therefore, the surrender of self must be our first and top priority. Our flesh wants whatsoever thing we are believing God for to appear on earth immediately, per our timetable. Flesh has no patience.

We must crucify all works of our flesh; for what we have not crucified can prevent us from having what we ask for. This is why it's important to have two in agreement (Matthew 18:19).

Where Are the Things
We Ask God for?

Remember Habakkuk 2:3-4, *"For still the vision awaits its time; it hastens to the end — it will not lie. If it seems slow, wait for it. It will surely come, it will not delay...the just shall live by his faith."* And by our patience. Our daily profession that we love Christ Jesus as Our Lord, and obey His commandments, activates His Word within us that we have what we ask for in His Name (John 14:13-14). We just need to keep saying it. Habakkuk 2:2 tells us, *"Write the vision down on tablets. Make it plain so that he who reads it will run."* We are kings on earth and our written declaration, signed with the signet ring — the Name of Jesus, makes our vision a king's decree. Jesus teaches us in Mark 11:24, *"You will have what you ask for — believe in your heart that you have received it."* Now put to memory what God inspired the prophet to write in Habakkuk 2:3, *"If it seems slow, wait for it. It will surely come; it will not delay."* Declaring it with our mouth and putting it in writing makes it a king's decree — all the more ours if we wait patiently for it to appear on earth, with faith in His Word to produce the thing we visualize, hope for, ask and believe God for, knowing that it will appear on earth as good.

Remember what Jesus taught us about binding and loosing things in Matthew 18:18-19. Whatever things we desire to have on earth must first be loosed in heaven — from Zion, so they can be transferred to earth. God has these things ready for us— but sometimes they are being held in captivity on earth by the forces of evil; or their arrival time has been unduly interrupted. When you place an order over the internet from Amazon, HSN, or wherever, it's not on your front porch that very moment. But it should arrive within a certain time frame. And, if we don't receive it, we can put a trace on it. So it is with things we declare are ours in the Spirit. Locate the thief. The things we declare must first be loosed from wherever they are— whether they are being held captive on earth or are being held up somewhere in the heavenlies while in transit from Zion. In Zion there is no evil. So, we must bind evil on earth and in the heavenlies to end such demonic stoppages, knowing that whatever we bind on earth is already bound in heaven (Matthew 18:18).

Sometimes it may take two in agreement to get uninterrupted transit from Zion or such things released from captivity on earth. God has shown us the creative force of our words. When two kings together bind evil by using the Word, a devastating consuming force is created, destroying evil as we speak (Ezekiel 28:17).

Seek Ye First the Kingdom of God

MATTHEW 6:33 "Seek ye first the Kingdom of God and His righteousness..."

Matthew 6:33 tells us what Jesus said about getting our needs met and receiving the desires of our heart: *"Seek ye first the Kingdom of God and His righteousness; and all these things will be yours as well."* This principle is a key to the Kingdom. This commandment by Christ Jesus makes the point. Our dominion over the fish of the sea, birds of the air, and over every living thing that moves on earth must first be established in Zion. When we have been established in Zion, God will establish us on earth. At that point we need not keep going to Zion asking and seeking God to help us exercise our dominion on earth. The door has already been opened for us. Why would we weary the Father with such trivia? We need to take Him at His Word and believe.

We Can Find God's Plan for Us in the Throne Room

When we marry and decide to have children, we pray and ask God to bless our union with fine, healthy children. Just like the vision we have of the children we hope for, the things we need and hope for each day must be first established in the Spirit; our dominion itself must also be first established in the Spirit. This is a decision that we must make. We must decide to be established in the land. The order of things is this: decide a thing in our heart to establish the vision, go to the Father in Zion, receive His blessing and approval to exercise our authority on earth, declare it done with our mouth — and wait for it to appear as "good" on the earth

(Genesis 1:31). We were created in the image of the Father and Son, and after their likeness. Just as God told the prophet Jeremiah, *"For I know the plans I have for you, says the Lord – plans for your welfare and not for evil, to give you a future and a hope. Then you will call upon Me and come and pray to Me, and I will hear you. You will seek Me and find Me when you seek Me with your whole heart"* (Jeremiah 29:11-13). This message was meant for us all. He has plans for us.

Man's dominion remained intact until the spirit man Adam surrendered it to satan, another spiritual being, whose sole intent was to control life on earth. Satan will try to tell us that we can't create, nor can we have what we hope for. He has already told us, "God doesn't mean what He says" (Genesis 3:4-5). But we know better. Jesus has given back to us the dominion Adam lost. We can now "create" things into existence. We have such creative capability because we are God-like spirits, a new creation in Christ Jesus. What seemed so impossible in the past when our old man ruled over us is available to us now. God has shown us how to use our spiritual senses and weapons of warfare to overcome the enemy.

Our Anointing as Kings and Priests Is Spiritual

Things of the flesh are contrary to things of the spirit. Our anointing as kings and priests is given to us because we are of our spiritual family tree— not because of how we are regarded by the world, or what position we might hold on earth, or who we think we are in man's eyes, or even who we might become in the future. We matter to God—body, soul and spirit. He establishes us in ministerial positions on earth.

Whether we have been formally ordained by the elders of a church or by some court— it is by God's choosing that we are His kings and priests on earth.

God instructed the prophet Samuel to anoint David as King of Israel many years before he was actually crowned on earth. And that anointing preserved the southern kingdom of Israel (House of Judah) throughout the reign of Solomon, long after the northern kingdom had fallen. But King Jeconiah (aka Jehoiachin, son of Jehoiakim) gave himself up to King Nebuchadnezzar and the Babylonians who had invaded the land. Jeconiah and his family were taken away to captivity together with most of the people of Israel, and enslaved by Nebuchadnezzar; he dethroned Jeconiah and appointed Jeconiah's uncle, Zedekiah, as a puppet king over the remnant of the people of Israel who remained in Jerusalem and Judea.

Solomon Broke Covenant with God

In the case of Jeconiah, only by God's grace and love for David had the southern kingdom (House of Judah) survived long after the northern kingdom had fallen. Centuries before when David's son Solomon married foreign wives, and he and some of his 700 wives and 300 concubines began worshiping other gods, God wrested the united kingdom away from Solomon's son Rehoboam and it became divided into the northern and southern kingdoms (I Kings 11:1-13), But when Jeconiah of the House of Judah abdicated his throne to Nebuchadnezzar and the Babylonians, where he remained in exile as long as he lived, surrendering himself and his family, his palace officials, together with 7,000 men of valor and 1,000 craftsmen, God removed the signet ring from Jeconiah's finger and his son (II Kings 24:8-16; Jeremiah 22:24-30). Zedekiah, Jeconiah's successor, appointed by Nebuchadnezzar, was little more than a status authority. Only when Zerubbabel, Jeconiah's grandson and a man of faith and courage arose among the people, who led His people back to Jerusalem, did God change His mind about the succession of the kingship and restored the signet ring of the House of Judah to the Davidian lineage.

Although Zedekiah is "officially" regarded as the last king of Israel, God had removed the signet ring from Jeconiah's finger; thus disestablishing the status authority of the Davidian Line of Kings at that time. Later, however, God anointed Jeconiah's grandson, Zerubbabel, as a Davidian king, and placed the signet ring on his finger, thus reestablishing the Davidian Lineage.. Zerubbabel was not a king in the world's eyes, but the governor of the Persian province of Judah who led a migration of over 42,000 Jews back to Jerusalem. God anointed Zerubbabel as king of the House of Judah, in the Spirit, just as He had done centuries earlier when the prophet Samuel communicated God's anointing as the King of Israel to a shepherd boy named David, even though Saul was physically sitting on the throne at the time. And God spoke unto the prophet Zechariah, as recorded in Zechariah 4:6, *This is the Word of the Lord unto Zerubbabel (whom I have anointed as king), saying, "Not by power, nor by might, but by My Spirit," saith the Lord* (Zechariah 4:6).

This same signet ring with God's anointing would be passed down spiritually to the Son of David, the Lion of Judah and our Lord and Savior, King Jesus Christ, under whose authority we have also been anointed as Davidian Kings in Zion with authority on earth. Because we have been grafted into this holy lineage (Romans 11:17), we are entitled to wear the signet ring of our Lord Jesus. We are entitled to use his Name.

The Status Authority of Kings on Earth Is Not the Anointing

The story of these kings and the signet ring gives us opportunity to search out the truth about spiritual authority. Bloodline and position, combined with physical power and might, is how the world recognizes authority. This is typically called status authority. But when we as children of God serve Him and obey His commandments, God establishes our spiritual authority in Zion and expects it to produce results on earth. When Christ Jesus baptizes us in the Holy Spirit He anoints us with spiritual power and authority to be used on earth. We can understand this gift from God when we examine spiritual dominion.

Such is like the adage, "Everything produces after itself." Applying a multiplication factor to this adage, in the beginning, when God told man to be fruitful and multiply (Genesis 1:28), He was speaking not only to children born of the physical union of two flesh bodies, but also of spiritual virtues and truths born of His Spirit. God intended for such to be found in generation after generation; beginning with Adam's children; and that every generation of his descendants would produce children in the spiritual image and likeness of God, just as Adam and Eve were created. And, from these roots, kings and priests were born.

Sadly, as the Apostle Paul writes to us in Second Thessalonians 3:2, ..."*not all men have faith.*" Beginning with Adam and Eve, God's children would allow spiritual attributes of evil to take root and destroy His plan for mankind. When this occurred, kings and priests God declared to have His power and authority on earth proved to be faithless offspring, unworthy to enjoy such blessings; and, ruling as evil powers, without the anointing of God, most brought evil upon their people and even lost their status authority — either by death at the hands of their own people or by allowing their people to be destroyed by foreign powers. Such leaders were usually destroyed. Through the ages, even until the present day, these same principles apply. God's eyes search to and fro, searching for men and women of God whose hearts are blameless toward Him — and who have the faith and courage to perform His will on earth (II Chronicles 16:9).

God establishes His kingship in us and multiplies our descendants. But we must beware of the things of this world. Adam's image and likeness changed when he and Eve chose to obey satan. Therefore, although we all have a perfect spirit when God places us in our mother's womb, we are immediately affected by the world around us — and we are changed. However, when we put on the mind of Christ, we learn what pleases God, and commit ourselves to carry out the commission Jesus has given to us (I Corinthians 2:13-16; Eph. 5:10; Matthew 28:18-20).

We Are No Longer Bound by the Law of Sin and Death

The Mosaic Law imposed physical regulations on the people. It was based upon a covenant of the flesh between Abraham and God requiring circumcision of all males. Obedience to the Law was required in the flesh; and disobedience required physical punishment. When Jesus was baptized in the Spirit by His Father at the outset of His ministry on earth, for Jesus, the New Covenant began. And Jesus completed the Old Covenant of the flesh while He was dying on the cross. His last words were, *"It is finished"*, before He gave up His Spirit (John 19:30).

We have crucified our proud, arrogant self with Him; and, when we confess our sins to the Father, the blood of His Son Jesus cleanses us of all unrighteousness; He is faithful and just, and will forgive our sins and cleanse us of all unrighteousness (I John 1:7-9). Therefore, we are no longer bound by the Law of Sin and Death; the wages of sin is death, but the free gift of God is eternal life in Christ Jesus our Lord (Romans 6:23 and 7:1-6).

The Body of Christ Lives Today

Satan may have thought that Jesus was out of his way when He was crucified at Calvary. But His disciples multiplied; and they began to pray together in one accord for the power of the Holy Spirit to come upon them just as He had promised (Acts 1:8). And, on the Day of Pentecost, 40 days after Christ Jesus ascended into heaven to be with His Father in Zion, the image and likeness of God was incarnated in the body of 120 true believers as they were gathered together in one place praying in one accord. Then there came the rush of a mighty wind; and all received the Baptism in the Holy Spirit from the Lord Jesus himself (Acts 2:1-4).

The early church would then grow from one, the Christ, to 120— on the strength of the blood of the Lamb who gave His life as a ransom for many (Mark 10:45)— and New Covenant man's trust in the Father's Word, as their testimonies proclaimed. Even to this very day the body of Christ continues to grow as we overcome evil (Revelation 12:11). The 120 would increase rapidly from that day to the countless number of believers of faith on earth today— confirming the Word of God given to Abraham centuries before," *As the dust of the earth if a man can number it will your seed be— as numerous as the stars in the sky* "(Genesis 13:16 & 15:5). We cannot count them.

We Are God's Offspring

Acts 17:28-29 tells us that we are God's offspring, for in Him we live and move. The Apostle Paul teaches us that we are also Abraham's spiritual offspring, and so we have all the promises that God made to Abraham (Galatians 3:16). Such a bountiful blessing. We can understand why God told him, *"By you, all the families on earth can bless themselves"* (Genesis 12:3). God intends for His faith, as found in Father Abraham to reap an hundredfold in us. Peter spoke this same faith when he said to Jesus, *"You are the Messiah, the Son of the Living God"* (Matthew 16:16). And we surely know how Jesus answered him, *"You are Peter; and on this rock I will build My church, and the gates of hell shall not prevail against it"* (Matthew 16:18).

God's Word Will Not Return to Him Empty

ISAIAH 55:11 "My Word that goes forth from My mouth will not return to Me empty; but they shall accomplish that which I purpose and profit the thing in which I sent it."

In the Spirit, we hear God the Father saying to His Son in the beginning, *"Let us create man in Our Own image, after Our likeness; and let them have dominion over the fish of the sea, the cattle, and over all the earth, and over every creeping thing that creeps upon the earth." And so He did, male and female He created them, and gave them dominion over every living thing that moves upon the earth"* (Genesis 1:26). Before He departed the earth, Jesus made certain that this powerful gift would be available to man once more. At the Last Supper, He proclaimed this gift to the eleven and to us: *"If a man loves Me, He will keep My Word, and My Father will love Him; and We will come to him and make Our home with him"* (John 14:23). Sinful Levitical priests could not restore man's image and likeness to God. So God the Father chose His Son to be our personal High Priest, One Who has walked the earth. He ordained Him.

Our High Priest Baptizes Us with Power and Authority

ISAIAH 61:1-3 "The Spirit of the Lord God is upon me. Because the Lord has anointed Me to bring good tidings to the afflicted; He has sent Me to bind up the brokenhearted, proclaim liberty to the captives and the opening of the prison for those who are bound; to proclaim the year of the Lord's favor, and the day of vengeance of our God; to comfort all who mourn, and grant to those who mourn in Zion the garment of praise that they might be called oaks of righteousness, the planting of the Lord, that He might be glorified."

The restoration of man to His creative state of dominion became possible for all whosoevers when Jesus returned to Zion after His crucifixion and resurrection. Of course, it is up to each of us to claim this restoration for ourselves. It is Our Lord Jesus who baptizes, arming us with His authority on earth, that is, His Signet Ring, removed from King Jeconiah by God centuries earlier, thus ending the Davidian line of kings. But God then gave the ring to Jeconiah's grandson, Zerubbabel, who would not have been royalty except that God anointed him to be His king, just as He has anointed Jesus to be King of kings (Haggai 2:23). We note here that the elders of Israel had anointed David as king over all of Israel, thus officially establishing the Davidian line of kings (II Samuel 5:3).

We Are Davidian Kings and Have the Right to the Name of Jesus

As told by the prophet Zechariah, when God removed the ring from Jeconiah's finger, in the Spirit, He transferred the power of David's kingdom from the "official" Davidian Line of kings to Christ Jesus— who then willed it to us. God did this to assure the world and the hierarchy of Christian denominations that He considers us as Jews, And God did this *not by power nor by might— but by my Spirit," saith the Lord of hosts* (Zechariah 4:6-10). He did it because, in His eyes, King Jesus wears the signet ring of God which He removed from Jeconiah; and Jesus has willed the ring to us— with instructions on its use. So, in order for us to wear the ring and exercise authority on earth, God grafted us into power. And Jesus has now willed His Signet Ring and kingly power to us, as declared by the Holy Spirit (John 16:13-15). We know that the ring is His Name; and He has given us permission to use His Name on earth (Matthew 18:18-20; John 14:13-14). Jesus has also given us the Banner of the Lion of Judah to carry with us into battle each day as a flag of victory over evil— so all citizens of Zion can see who we are (Revelation 5:5). We carry His banner in our hearts.

"Put On the Whole Armor of God"

EPHESIANS 6:10-11   Be strong in the Lord and the strength of His might. Put on the whole armor of God, that you may be able to stand against the wiles of the devil.

It would seem that with all the magnanimous resourcefulness God has given to us, there should be no reason for concern, anxiety, and certainly not fear. We should know the importance of all aspects of our spiritual authority on earth, and how to attain and exercise our God-given power to move mountains on earth. Remember, our battle on earth is waged against spiritual powers of darkness in heavenly places. Because our flesh often becomes frustrated with our circumstances, we are tempted to wing it on our own. Big mistake— we cannot. Our flesh is forgetful, undependable, and weak. We must fight evil, spirit to spirit. When we do, we realize satan is a defeated loudmouth. Besides, the battle is God's— the victory is ours.

From the very moment the 120 were baptized in the Holy Spirit they were no longer mere wandering sojourners— they were ambassadors on a mission. They now had the whole armor of God they needed as kings to go into battle for the Kingdom of God and King Jesus. And to stand against the strong man— girded with truth, wearing the breastplate of righteousness, shod with the equipment of the gospel of peace, taking the shield of faith, putting on the helmet of salvation, and adorned for battle with the sword of the Spirit— which is the Word of God; and remembering to pray in the Spirit always (Ephesians 6:11-18).

We Are Fighting a Spiritual War

From the Day of Pentecost after Jesus ascended forward to the present day, the power of the Holy Spirit on earth has multiplied many times over as the number of anointed full gospel Christians has become innumerable. We continue to experience the hundredfold return. The Holy Spirit has empowered the disciples of Christ Jesus throughout this New Covenant Age to battle the principalities, the powers, the world rulers of the present day darkness, and the spiritual hosts of wickedness in heavenly places (Ephesians 6:12). This war was not confined to the early church, but has been ongoing, from generation to generation thereafter, including our own— and which will continue until the end of the Age. Jesus baptizes us in the Holy Spirit to arm us with His power. By using our new prayer language which is included as a sign that we have received this powerful Baptism— praying in the Spirit, we have a complete set of armor to use in battle. Thus, Christ Jesus Our Shepherd, who knows first-hand what we face in this life, completes our spiritual armor so we can show ourselves to the enemy with renewed confidence. No more hiding. Our armor buoys our soul to give us the courage to take our position. Remember, just as God told King Jehoshaphat and the people in II Chronicles 20:15-19, when the king was confronted by a mighty enemy army, the battle against the enemy is God's and the victory is ours. The bleeding need not be— our Savior Jesus has already shed enough blood; and if satan dares to test us— which he surely will, we need only remember that the Lamb of God shed His blood as a ransom for us all. For us to shed more blood or anguish in fear is unacceptable to God. Such would only be a sign of our doubt and unbelief. Jesus defeated death once and for all time.

We Will Do All We Need to Do to Stand Against Satan

We are committed and determined to stand against the deceitful wiles of the devil (Eph. 6:13-14). And because we continue in this commitment, we will stand. God baptizes us with fire to remove the chaff from us— thus strengthening us to endure the trials and temptations God allows to come.

Ambassadors Well Armed
To Fight and Stand Against Evil

II CORINTHIANS 5:20 "We are ambassadors for Christ reconciling the world to God..."

As *City Dwellers*, we are ambassadors for the Kingdom of God and Our Lord Jesus. Jesus has anointed us for heavy duty because we are His friends— He loves us and needs us to carry on His work on earth. So the Father allows us to be tempted, and for trials of our faith to come— in order to build us up for even tougher battles as we mature in Christ Jesus, and prove to Him we can handle greater ambassadorial responsibilities. As ambassadors, we have been commissioned as one in Him and the Father, just as He prayed at the Last Supper (John 17:20-23).

We serve under our Lord God Jehovah, with the authority of Christ Jesus and the Word of His Power. By using His Name, we know that we have His signet ring; we have His Word of Assurance that He will never leave us or forsake us (Matthew 28:20). And we have His promise that the empowerment of the Holy Spirit and His gifts are available to us by accepting and receiving the Baptism in the Holy Spirit. And we have the grace of Our Lord Jesus and His patience and toleration of our failures, as He helps us pass the baptism by fire; the love of God the Father, as He sends His angels to minister to our needs (Hebrews 1:14), opens the windows of heaven to shower us with His blessings (Malachi 3:10), and sees our good works of faith that we declare and proclaim. They produce what we envision and hope for as good on earth, just as He declared in the beginning (Genesis 1:31); and the fellowship of the Holy Spirit abiding in us, as he equips us with weapons of warfare and counsels us in secret to be all we can be in and through our service and leadership to our brethren in the world.

Our High Priest Has Also
Armed Us with His Power

It is our Lord and High Priest Jesus who arms us with His power — His Word of Power, of which He shares with all of us as joint heirs with Him of the Kingdom of God — and by which He holds up the universe as He reflects the glory of the Father (Hebrews 1:2-3; John 17:22; Romans 8:17). And Our High Priest baptizes us with the power of the Holy Spirit that we need to battle satan on earth (Matthew 3:11).

It is our Lord Jesus who graciously showers us with His grace (II Corinthians 13:14), as He helps us through the baptism of fire He has also allowed. (Matthew 3:11). This baptism assures us that we can pass through the fire of persecution and the habitation of wild beasts without being consumed or torn apart. And, through it all, God never allows us to be tempted beyond our capacity to endure (I Cor. 10:13).

We Have Excellent Weapons of War

Our most important task is to stay focused on the goal line. Remember especially to put on the whole armor of God when confronting the devil. Knowing the Word of God and how to apply it to our situation and circumstances is essential to our success. The Word of God is the Sword of the Holy Spirit, a valuable component of our battle armor (Ephesians 6:17). Therefore, we cannot be careless or slack, nor can our meditation be cursory. We must prepare ourselves for battle; and God tells us how to win the victory in the Spirit. We cannot defeat evil in the flesh. If we try to defeat Him by our own power and might, we soon realize the futility of our battle.

A Battlefield Requirement:
Be Versed in the Word

II TIMOTHY 3:16   All scripture is inspired by God and profitable for teaching, for reproof, for correction, and for training in righteousness...

While all scripture is worthy, when we read the Bible in the flesh we embarrass ourselves and God. Just as we must worship God in Spirit and truth (John 4:20-24), we must also meditate in the Word in Spirit and truth. Meditation in God's Word is worship. Psalm 19:14 so instructs us: *"Let the words of my mouth and the meditation of my heart be acceptable in Thy sight, O Lord — my Rock and my Redeemer."* When we fail to include God in our meditation time, we are reducing His

Word to little more than a social studies history book— and we are allowing our flesh to try to make sense of God's inspired Word. What good does that do us?

A good friend of mine once told me, "When I became a Christian I read the Bible from Genesis to Revelation and I didn't get a thing out of it." Of course not. It cannot be read as a novel or mere history book. He's gone on to be with the Lord now, and surely the Lord has assigned Him a bit of study in the Word. When we don't include God in our meditation and inspired reading in the Bible, we allow our flesh to control our meditation.

We Know Better Than to
Allow Satan to Control Anything

The word, *"knowledge"* in Hosea 4-6 almost immediately witnesses with our flesh, and we think of "chapter and verse" as crucial to our understanding of what the Father is teaching us. So we begin using our physical senses which is what our flesh understands. But what does the Father intend for *City Dwellers* to understand in this passage? If we substitute a word or two, we can find a better way to address the problem. Better phraseology may be, *"My people are destroyed for their inability to apply the wisdom and insight I have given them to their situation and circumstances."* Now we are looking at something that is well beyond what our flesh understands. And we immediately look at the spiritual realm, at what God is teaching us in spirit and truth. We now realize that we will need to use our spiritual senses— which is what God intends for His people to use. No, he does not intend for the world to understand the meaning of the verse; but He surely wants us to know the passage well. The better our ability to apply the principle to the situations and circumstances in our own lives, the more abundant our lives will become.

Proverbs 29:18 teaches us, *Where there is no vision, the people perish.* We also need to understand this scripture, so it requires close scrutiny. The words, "vision" and "perish" both need clarification. "Vision" is meant to be a spiritual word in this verse: we see in the Spirit what we hope for manifest as "good" in the physical earth. This is exactly how God created things on earth: He saw everything first in His Spirit before he declared them to be manifest as "good" on earth (Genesis 1:31). We must see the things we hope for with our spiritual eyes, and declare them into existence on earth before we can expect them to appear on earth. Lest we fall into a flesh trap by saying, "Seeing is believing", a better word for "vision" in this passage is probably "revelation". We know the word, "revelation", is a spiritual word— so let's substitute it for the word, "vision".

The word, "perish", in this passage is also intended as a "spiritual" word in its application.

God is telling us that we must be able to use our faith and our spiritual senses; and apply spiritual principles in our situation and circumstances to achieve what we hope for, and begin living the abundant life on earth in this age. The things we "visualize" in the spirit realm are not on earth, but in Zion waiting for us to claim them.

How Was Daniel Delivered from the Lions' Den?

> DANIEL 6:19-23 At the break of day the king arose and went in haste to the den of lions... he cried out in anguish, "O Daniel, servant of the living God, has your God Whom you serve continually, been able to deliver you from the lions?" Then Daniel said to the king, "O king, live forever. My God sent his angel to shut the lions' mouths, and they have not hurt me, because I was found blameless before Him and also before you, O king. I have done no wrong." Then the king was exceedingly glad.

Daniel was delivered from the lions' den because He trusted God. The story of Daniel in the Lions Den is quite familiar to all of us and an appropriate way of showing us the importance of trusting God — no matter how difficult the circumstances may be for us at any given time in our life here on earth. As we revisit this story, we need to pinpoint the circumstances that caused him to be thrown in the den. While the Jewish nation was in captivity by the Babylonians, Daniel and his three friends —

Shadrach, Meshach, and Abednego, were servants of Babylonian King Nebuchadnezzar. They had earned the king's favor because of their keen minds. Over time Daniel had been given increasing authority within the kingdom — so much so that other men in authority became exceedingly jealous of Daniel and plotted to have him killed.

Knowing Daniel would never worship another god other than the Most High, the jealous bunch devised a way to do it. They simply asked the king to issue a decree calling for a 30-day period of time during which any petition by the king's subjects could be presented only to King Nebuchadnezzar. And anyone of the king's subjects who disobeyed the king's decree would be thrown into a den of lions as his punishment. The king signed the order, but of course Daniel refused to obey — and the conspirators reported him to the king for the king's disposition.

Now the king was very fond of Daniel and sought to exempt Daniel from execution. However, the conspirators reminded the king that the law of the land prohibited him from breaking or rescinding his decree. So the king could not sleep and was understandably worried about Daniel's demise. When morning came, he hurried to the den, only to find an unharmed Daniel. God had closed the mouths of the lions.

We Have Nothing to Fear

PSALM 34:19 Many are the afflictions of the righteous, but God delivers us from them all.

Today we sometimes find ourselves in the lions' den with danger all about us. In the natural, there just seems to be no way out. Jesus has already paid the price the enemy exacted from him when he was in control of things. Don't let him fool you— He's been defeated. But we must remember that we are undergoing a baptism by fire— and must learn to trust God for deliverance. God told the prophet Isaiah, *"Fear not, for I have redeemed you; I have called you by name; you are Mine. When you pass through the waters, I will be with you; and through the rivers, they shall not overwhelm you. When you walk through the fire, you shall not be burned, and the flame shall not consume you; for I am the Lord your God, the Holy One of Israel, Thy Savior"* (Isaiah 43:1-3).

"My Words Shall Never Pass Away"

Jesus stripped the devil of His authority on earth at Calvary. But with His crucifixion, our requirement to help Him carry His cross began. Often we tend to forget that. When we are arrayed in our full battle armor, the odds of us enduring frontal assaults from the devil as well as refusing to fall prey to his deceitful promises of earthly riches, are infinitesimally improved because of what Jesus has done for us. We just need to remember God's assurance in Isaiah 43;

and believe the words of Jesus in Matthew 28:20, *"I am with you always – even to the close of the age."* One more point needs to be emphasized here. Jesus also promises us that His words will abide: *"Heaven and earth shall pass away, but My Words shall never pass away"* (Matthew 24:35; Mark 13:31; Luke 21:33). We find this promise in three gospel accounts no less. This should be good enough for all true believers to know that no part of our battle armor has passed away. We can take comfort knowing that Jesus will help us carry the cross and help us discharge the commission He has given to us. Sometimes that's difficult when we hear contrary messages from the pulpit; or denominations of the church indoctrinate us to believe all gifts of the Spirit have passed away. Satan enjoys such teachings because they enable him to target our flesh and invade our soul. You hear from seminary-educated shepherds that there are no prophets today. Well, Jesus was a prophet and at the Last Supper He gave us all that He had – including His ability to prophesy.

6

We Are A Chosen Generation

I PETER 2:9 You are a chosen generation, a royal priesthood, a holy nation, God's Own people.

II CORINTHIANS 5:17 If any man is in Christ, he is a new creation. The old has passed away; the new has come.

There are but two generations in God's journal to identify the relationship of God and man: (1) the Old Covenant Generation, including all generations of Adam and "Pre-Noahic" generations— as well as Noah's generations; and all peoples who lived under the Abrahamic and Mosaic Covenants; and (2) the New Covenant Generation of the blood of Jesus Christ. Sometimes we really have to go to Zion to escape what seems to be a reality that we are "earthlings". We are not. The devil wants us to believe that we are citizens of the earth and desires to keep us in the flesh. But we are spirits— housed in a body of flesh because the earth's atmosphere and gravity requires us to have weight in a "body of matter".

We are really heavenly *City Dwellers*, and God wants us to know the absolute truth about where we dwell and where we temporarily reside.

Isaiah 30:19 tells us the truth: We dwell in Zion at Jerusalem. The Bible identifies the generations of the Old and New Covenant— or Old and New Testament people, as physically living on the earth. However, for clarification, we may find it easier to use these chronological descriptors: (1) Pre-Adamic Age (before Adam); (2) Noahic Age; (3) Old Covenant Age; (4) New Covenant Age— in which we now live; and (5) Age after Christ— or, for all believers, the Age of Jubilee in Eternity. Moreover, I Peter 2:5-9 identifies us as *living stones, a chosen generation.* This scripture unquestionably refers to the New Covenant Generation as a spiritual generation empowered by the anointing of the Holy Spirit. So we should not be confused. We are spirits; so we should know that God does not measure time the way we do— He looks on the readiness of a man's heart to receive Him; and what man is doing with the gifts he has given him before identifying him as an Old Covenant or New Covenant man. The Apostle Paul writes in II Corinthians 5:17, *"If any man be in Christ He is a new creation — the old has passed away, the new has come"*. Most true believers are going through the baptism by fire, as they put on the mind of Christ. When the Holy Spirit enters into us and begins teaching our spirit man, we can no longer think carnally without being instantly convicted. As Jesus tells us, it is impossible to serve two masters (Matthew 6:24).

Using Spiritual Descriptors to Identify All Ages

I Peter 2:9 also helps us to identify all ages by spiritual descriptors. Why? Our earthly father "fathered" our flesh and bones— and our mother "birthed" our flesh and bones. But God made us from His Own Spirit— from His Son's Spirit. This is why we know that we were created as perfect— in the exact image and likeness of himself and His Son Jesus. In using such a measuring stick, we are able to group all generations of prehistoric life— dinosaurs, birds, fish, prehistoric mammals and the so-called "cave man", as having existed during a Pre-Adamic Age (before Adam), when the earth was void of plant and animal life, certainly not a man in God's image and after His likeness, as we know and recognize man today; and occurring many millennia before God created the first man, but while Lucifer and his demonic army walked upon and occupied the earth.

Every living thing evil touched became accursed— including the dust of the earth. This curse fell upon Adam's perfect spirit when he sinned against God. This curse fell upon all of his descendants until Christ Jesus came to earth, was crucified, dead, and buried— was resurrected to life by the Father, and appeared to His disciples and the women on several occasions before He ascended into heaven where He now sits at the right hand of the Father. He paid the price for the eternal redemption of believers with

His own blood. This was the ransom the devil required before our release could be attained.

The Family Tree of God's People

MATTHEW 1:2-16   Abraham was the father of Isaac... and Jacob the father of Joseph, the husband of Mary, of whom Jesus was born, who is called Christ.

LUKE 3:23-38   Jesus when He began His ministry, was about thirty years of age, being the son (as was supposed) of Joseph...the son of Nathan, the son of David...the son of God.

Before God inspired me to write this book, I admit that I never spent much time studying genealogical records. All of us have a family tree, and throughout the generations of both the Old Testament and the New Testament, the sins of Adam have shown up in our genes. Geneticists have determined that through the generations certain inherited defects of the flesh have hindered mankind in one way or another. Their findings confirm the Word as recorded for us in Haggai 2:13, telling us that even the physical contact of clean flesh by unclean flesh will contaminate clean flesh. Still, the history of mankind, by bloodline, can be traced back through the generations to Adam— whether before the birth of Christ Jesus or thereafter. Matthew 1:2-17 traces His genealogy back for some 32 generations— to Abraham; however, it is really the family tree of his stepfather, Joseph.

Luke 3:23-38 traces our Lord's genealogy back to the beginning, to God the Father— which indeed is more accurate, especially since this genealogical record is really the family tree of His mother Mary. Both historical records represent physical facts— where and when Jesus' ancestors "landed" on earth— in the flesh. But Jesus is the child of the Virgin Mary. God the Father Himself is He who begat Jesus. In fact, John 8:58 records Jesus declaring, *"Before Abraham was born, I am."* And we know that Jesus is our Creator because in Colossians 1:15-16, we read, Jesus is the first-born of all creation; for in Him all things were created, in heaven and on earth.

So it is that when we refer to the family tree of our Lord Jesus, we are concerned primarily with how we qualify for inclusion. The birth registry found in Matthew 1:2-17 is a record of available physical facts— for Joseph's bloodline, true as far as the record goes, as is Luke 3:23-38 for Mary's bloodline. We take note as we study these accounts that both Joseph and Mary were descendants of David— Joseph, by David's son, Solomon; and Mary, by David's son, Nathan. However, both appear to be descendants of Zerubbabel whom God chose to wear His signet ring (Haggai 2:23). This becomes important as we legally justify who we are.

Our Names Are Listed in Jesus' Genealogy

ISAIAH 58:12 "You shall raise up the foundations of many generations; you shall be called the repairer of the breach, the restorer of streets to dwell in."

Since we have been born of His Spirit and washed in His blood, we now have the privilege of entering our own names on His family tree as sons and daughters of God in Christ, who established our righteousness— by our faith, the faith of Abraham, by covenant; our kingship of David, by covenant; and our royal priesthood of Jesus Christ, by covenant. We know that God has given us a legal right to membership in the Family of God— by His adoption of us as His children (Romans 8:14-17)— thereby entitling us to be listed on Abraham's physical genealogy, from whom David and Jesus were born. And, because of our belief in Jesus as Lord, we know we belong to Him spiritually— and that no curse can fall upon the spiritual genealogy of Jesus Christ. We are redeemed from the curse (Galatians 3:13). But if we are going to readily accept our spiritual genealogy with gladness, we must surrender our carnal desires. We have a way to Zion, but we can't get there if we are still living in and by the flesh. We need to realize that sooner or later such a life takes us into desert wastelands where we may wander for another forty years with our soul fainting within us just as what occurred when the Israelites rejected the opportunity given to them to enter the promised land (Psalm 107:4-7; Numbers 14).

The Abrahamic Covenant— Our Family Tree of Righteousness

MATTHEW 1:1 The book of the genealogy of Jesus Christ, the son of David, the son of Abraham.

GENESIS 22:18 "And in your offspring shall all the nations of the world bless themselves."

A close examination of Matthew 1:1 lets us see quickly that this verse lists an ancestral line for Jesus of only two people— Abraham and David, and therefore differs from the complete physical genealogies of Jesus as contained in Matthew 1:2 and Luke 3:23. Why? Because the genealogy in this passage is not physical or genetical. It is the spiritual genealogy of Christ Jesus— and redeemed from the curse of Adam or the Law of Moses. Let's examine the Abrahamic Covenant, also regarded as our Faith Covenant with God.

We Have Inherited God's Promises to Abraham

We know that by faith we are redeemed from the curse because it is confirmed in the Word (Galatians 3:13). In Ezekiel 18:20, we read that a man's righteousness is credited to him— that in God's eyes, he does not inherit the sins of his father nor is the righteous son infected by the sins of his sinful mother. Note the word, "righteous". This refers to the workings of faith by all believers who see the thing they hope for in the spirit realm, and know they are going to receive it, and use their faith to ensure that it appears on earth. This explanation gives us a much better understanding of the Abrahamic Covenant. This covenant was established by Abraham's faith in and obedience to God's Word. Abraham's faith was reckoned to him as righteousness (Genesis 15:6; Romans 4:3). Because of Abraham's righteousness, God told him that he would be the Father of Many Nations— nations whose people would live by faith. Jesus prayed the Father in John 17:22-23 at the Last Supper, that His disciples and all of us who live by our faith in Him would be perfectly one— one holy nation, one generation, as proclaimed by the Apostle Peter in I Peter 2:9. Abraham is considered to be the Father of Our Faith.

A Study of Physical Genealogy

When we study genealogy from a strictly physical or genetical point of view, we bypass the faith realm of the New Covenant. Our study becomes a mere historical survey— with one exception. Genetically speaking, we are bound to inherit the genes of our ancestors. Such an approach to genealogy requires that all of us are bound to live under the curse of Adam. Not so. Anyone living under the Old Covenant lived under a genetic curse that the sins of the fathers will be visited upon the sons for a thousand generations (Exodus 20:5-6; Deuteronomy 5:9-10). But the New Covenant Generation has been redeemed from the curse. The blood of Jesus wiped away the genetic stigma of Adam that plagued Old Covenant people for centuries. Some still believe it to be true— for they cannot accept God's Word that the curse has been washed away by the power in His blood. This erroneous belief discounts faith as the primary factor in determining the life span of man. Such erroneous thinking pervades our medical history, as required by physicians and life insurance underwriters; and makes us prone to accept the predicted probability that we will live a long or relatively short time on earth.

"As a Man Thinks, So He Is"

We cannot do a thing about our ancestral family history. If we persist in thinking that we are bound by our genetic weaknesses, it will be so for us (Proverbs 23:7). Yet, by faith, we know that by the blood of Jesus we have been sanctified, justified and transfused, can live 120 years (Genesis 6:3), have been predestined to be His adopted children, have received the spirit of adoption, and have been grafted into His family tree (Romans 11:17; Ephesians 1:5). It would seem that the spiritual genetics make a difference in the length of our days as does what we believe.

We Are Children of the Promise

DEUTERONOMY 14:2 God has chosen us to be a holy people unto Himself— for His Own possession, above all the peoples on the face of the earth.

The petitions of the Father that Jesus made in prayer while He was here on earth translate into God's promises. He assures us that we have been made children of the promise God made to Abraham, Isaac, and Jacob— that their descendants would be like the dust of the earth...as the stars of heaven...and that by them all the families of the earth shall bless themselves (Gen. 12:3; 15:5; 26:4; 28:14). The confirmation of this promise can be found in Deu. 14:1-2; we are the children of the Lord our God...and He has chosen us to be a holy people unto Himself, above all the peoples on the face of the earth.

Our Citizenship in Zion Today Is Conditional

However, there is one condition to our assertion that we are God's children and given permission to be in our homeland today. God the Father has given us the assurance that we have eternal life. But what about the abundant life on earth today? That depends on our faith in God's Word. Jesus said that we can have the abundant life on earth today. He is there now. And we can go in and out of Zion, even into the Father's throne room, and find pasture in Jerusalem (John 10:9-10). This is a promise to whosoever believes. Do we trust Him? As given to us by the Apostle Paul in Romans 8:14 when he writes, *for all who are led by the Spirit of God are children of God.*

Therefore, we who believe and profess Jesus Is Lord continually by the word of our testimony — our profession of faith, are God's true children; and are welcome to come to Zion today. Whether we choose to accept this truth or not, because of the love of God in Christ Jesus, we are God's Chosen Generation of New Covenant believers. We dare not miss out on all His promises. Our enemy would have us believe that God's promises and special endowments of spiritual gifts were given to a previous generation; and that nearly all of the anointing of Jesus and the early Christians has passed away. He tries to convince us, "Sorry, but you are not among the privileged few." What a lie. Of course, if we believe this to be true, we are powerless to fight against evil and satan knows it. He would have us unworthy of the Holy Spirit who lives within us and incapable of allowing Him to empower us to do God's will in and for us. God has chosen to favor us. We must use our spiritual senses to trace our spiritual family tree. Our mindset and reliance on our physical senses as our knowledge base makes the foregoing discussion hard to accept. We have pictures and snapshots on display in our own homes together with memorabilia to reflect four and five generations of our own families. When we think of generations in the natural, our physical senses always think of our own family tree. In the Bible, we think of who begat who— recorded for us in Genesis 5 as Adam's Generations; Genesis 6:9-10 as Noah's Generations; Genesis 11:10-32 as Shem's and Terah's Generations; and in several other places for the purpose of tracing genealogies— such as our Lord's genealogy in Matthew 1 and Luke 3; or determining who lived when or who settled where during periods of Israel's captivity and the restoration of Jerusalem. However, ancestral studies do not help us understand man's relationship with God.

Jesus Claimed Us as
His Own in the Beginning

Jesus claimed us as one generation in the beginning. When God the Father made us in His Own image and likeness, many believers also envision that He separated our spirits from the darkness— to be awakened at his time certain, *"under the apple tree"* while our mother was in travail (Song of Solomon 8:5). While He was still in the flesh on earth, Jesus prayed for us who are also in the flesh on earth to be one in Him because we are all one in God's eyes. When God created us, He declared our dominion over all the earth (Genesis 1:26-28). His proclamation means that we have been called by God to play an integral role in bringing Christ Jesus back to rule on earth while we are still in the flesh. He is now in the process of choosing the New Covenant Generation— one made up solely of committed whosoevers God needs to establish His Kingdom on earth during the current New Covenant Age. He is doing it today.

We know that we are "those who believe in Him through their word"— the chosen ones to whom Jesus promised to send the Holy Spirit. At the Last Supper Jesus declared to us what He so fervently desires, saying, *"all that the Father has is Mine; therefore I said that the Holy Spirit will take what is Mine and give it to you"* (John 16:15). John 17:20-24 tells us at the Last Supper before his arrest, Jesus prayed for all who are the New Covenant Generation: *"Father, I do not pray for these (eleven) only, but for all of those who believe in Me through their word, that they may all be one even as We are one; that they may be in Us, I in them and Thou in Me, that they may become perfectly one, so that the world may know that Thou hast sent Me and has loved them even as Thou hast loved Me. Father, I desire that they also, whom Thou hast given Me, may be with Me where I am, to behold My glory which Thou hast given Me in Thy love for Me before the foundation of the world."*

The question we must all ask ourselves is, "How committed am I to assure God that He can depend on me to become *'perfectly one'* in Him?" When we can answer this question in our hearts, we are ready to respond to the question God asks in Isaiah 6:8, "Whom shall I send, and who will go for Us? And I said, "Here I am, send me."

Are We Reigning as Kings on Earth Today?

I CORINTHIANS 4:8 "Already you are filled. Already you have become rich. Without us you have become kings. And would that you did reign, so that we may share the rule with you."

We are God's kings and lords on earth today. He urges us to reign as such in I Corinthians 4:8, II Timothy 2:12, and Revelation 5:10. These verses also confirm our charge— we must reign as kings in order for God's Word to accomplish what He declared it to do in the beginning— to prosper His Word. And when we prosper His Word, we give thanksgiving to our Lord Jesus who died for us— and we glorify Him. In Genesis 12:3 we hear God telling Abraham, *"I will bless those who bless you, and him who curses you I will curse; and by you all the nations of the world will bless themselves."* When we praise and worship the Father, we glorify His Son and bless ourselves. But when we don't, by our own abstention, we praise and worship worldly things. It's hard to accept, but whatever we think about so we are (Proverbs 23:7). An even bigger challenge is this: How can we take possession of and occupy our own promised land if we cannot or will not reign?

Reestablishing Our Citizenship in Zion

II CORINTHIANS 5:17 If any man be in Christ, he is a new creation.

We were surely birthed in Zion by God the Father in Zion; and lest we forget, we are spirits. But a lot changed after God put us in our mother's womb. He gave us a body of flesh and bones— and a soul with a spiritual mind capable of thinking, decision-making and expressing our emotions. And, because Adam gave up his dominion on earth over all living things that move upon the earth to a fallen angel, the perfect earth God created in the beginning became polluted; and our perfect spirits entered into a cruel, sinful world where demonic forces had taken up residence— and we were battered by the wind and the waves of a stormy sea.

We began to think like the world thinks, and act according to however our flesh demanded— which was often contrary to God's perfect will. In short, our spirit man became intimidated by the strong man of the world and his henchmen; and we became carnal and sinful people in need of a complete cleansing and restoration.

Our God Makes a Way
When There Is No Way

Yet, God is not about to abandon us. He called out our name— and we heard Him calling. We came to Him, and He chose us to do His work. And He began to build up our spirit man with His Word, and to reconstruct our damaged character. Still, we needed to become innocent again in order to have fellowship with Him in the Holy City of Zion. This required us to be born again (John 3:1-7). So, just as He did for His Old Covenant people when He brought them out of Egypt with a mighty hand and outstretched arm (Psalm 136:12), and made a way for them to escape across the Red Sea when there was no way— a loving and merciful God made a way for us to be with Him. By the miraculous birth of a child named Jesus, born of a virgin and lying in a manger (Luke 2:8-14) to be worshiped by millions of God's people through over 2,000 years, and by His cleansing blood and a public statement of our belief in Him as the Christ— His Son, God made a way for man to spend eternity in Zion (John 3:16).

Jesus Became the Way for Us
to Enter Zion Now

JOHN 14:6 Jesus said, "I am the Way, the Truth and the Life. No one comes to the Father but by Me."

Jesus wants those of us who have surrendered all of ourselves to Him and the Kingdom of God to be with Him where He is (John 10:9 and 17:24). So,

Jesus himself became the Way to Zion (John 14:6). And yet again, God made a way when there was no way. But this time, defying all imaginable possibilities, God gave New Covenant believers access to Himself in Zion, all because of Jesus. And, as prophesied in Isaiah 35, God constructed a spiritual highway, reserved for New Covenant believers who truly believe that they have been redeemed by the blood of the Lamb of God, Christ Jesus, that He shed at Calvary.

Only those of us who believe that God paid the ransom for our release from bondage with His Own blood shall ever walk upon this highway where we are brought by the Holy Spirit to meet Jesus himself. But we shall return again and again to our homeland on Mount Zion— now, in this age and time. Yes, we will spend eternity with Him there. But for now Jesus intends for us to continue His work on earth—first, Jerusalem, then Judea, and then Samaria, and then the whole world, until indeed, He calls us home to all of His Holy Mountain for eternity.

Zion Is Our Filling Station

When we see Jesus today, He shall be meeting us on the highway (Isaiah 35); and on to Zion we shall go, hand-in-hand with our Lord, singing and praising the Father. And when we arrive we shall surely enjoy visiting with the heavenly host— and, especially entering into the Father's throne room, and visiting with both the Father and Son, receiving both the strength and courage we need to confront evil on earth. While there in His presence we present our petitions and communicate freely with the Father— and receive instructions on what specific tasks He desires for us to fulfill before we return to Zion yet again; and we know if He hears us, we have what we asked for (Psalm 91:15; I John 5:14-15).

City Dwellers,
Jesus Awaits Our Arrival

With all God has done for us— especially to give us access to Him, today, and for eternity, we should be eager to comply with whatever citizenship regulations are required for us to reenter God's Holy City of Zion, enjoy immediate access to His holy mountain— and, most importantly, see Christ Jesus Our Lord and freely enter the Father's throne room with Him and at His invitation. So, although we are "natives" of Zion, as "earthlings" we know we don't deserve such a reentry. But, because we are His friends, His brethren— and His bride, for whom Jesus gave up His life, we have this access. Jesus prayed the Father to give us the Holy Spirit, the Spirit of the Father and Himself— so that we might dwell with Him and the Father in Zion today while we carry on His work on earth just as He commanded. We have it because He prayed the Father, proclaiming our citizenship rights and privileges to go into Zion and come out again while we are on earth (John 14:12-24; 17:20-26).

We cannot do His work without protected daily communication with our husband Christ Jesus, and getting the strength we need from Zion to battle the enemy on earth. And Jesus needs and expects each of us to carry out the commission He has given to us in Jerusalem, that is, in our own Jerusalem on earth first— and beyond, as we are so led by the Holy Spirit. Therefore, because of Jesus' intercession with the Father on our behalf, we can seek the Father's face. We want to be with our husband Jesus now; and we are eager to comply with whatever citizenship requirements that must be met.

City Dwellers, Our Mission Is Clear

MATTHEW 28:18-20 "And Jesus came and said to them, "All authority in heaven and earth has been given to Me. Go therefore, and make disciples of all nations, baptizing them in the Name of the Father, and of the Son, and of the Holy Spirit..."

LUKE 9:1-6 And Jesus called the twelve together; and gave them power and authority over all demons and to cure diseases, and He sent them out to preach the Kingdom of God and to heal. And He said to them, "Whatever house you enter, stay there, and from there depart; and wherever they do not receive you, shake off the dust from your feet as a testimony against them." And they departed and went through the villages, preaching the gospel and healing everywhere.

What are the basic rules for accepting and keeping Matthew 28:18-20? We hear the voice of our Lord calling us to serve and lead the children of God who are being called to Kingdom work. To accept the charge of such a great commission, we cannot remain in the innocent ignorance of our childhood years. Before we can discharge our commission, we must receive the Baptism in the Holy Spirit and go to Zion to check our battle armor and get the direction and strength we need to get our assignments done. Jesus established the pattern for our discipleship when He empowered the twelve, sending them into the towns and villages— giving them authority over evil spirits and diseases; and charging them to heal the sick and preach the Kingdom of God (Luke 9:1-6). Later, He anointed seventy other disciples and likewise sent them out with similar power and authority. When they returned, they reported to Jesus that even the demons were subject to them in His Name (Luke 10:1-17). Today He likewise empowers us and prepares us for our service. He needs our total commitment and obedience.

Are We Ready for the Cost of Our Discipleship?

A self-examination is a pre-requisite for citizenship in Zion so we can determine and declare our own maturity level before we begin to discharge our commissioned duties on earth. Christ Jesus wants us to be His ambassadors for the Kingdom of God. Just as He did during His ministry on earth for His twelve disciples (Luke 9) and the seventy others (Luke 10) he desires to send us into the towns and villages to proclaim the Kingdom of God; and to heal and drive out demons in His name. Jesus baptizes us in the Holy Spirit just as the Father baptized Him (Matthew 3:11-12); and arms us with His power and authority (Matthew 28:18-20; John 14:12; Acts 1:8). Jesus knows exactly where we are in our Christian walk. He yearns for us to be empowered by the Holy Spirit so we can enjoy the fullness of the abundant life here on earth— today, in this age.

What the Abundant Life
Really Means for Us

MARK 10:28-30 Then Peter said unto Him, "Lo, we have left all and have followed Thee." And Jesus answered and said, "Truly I say unto you, there is no one who has left house, or brothers, or sisters, or father, or mother, or wife, or children, or lands, for My sake, and the gospel's, who will not receive a hundredfold now in this time— houses and brothers, and sisters, and mothers, and children, and lands, with persecutions, and in the age to come eternal life."

Jesus teaches us in John 10:10 that the devil comes only to steal our goods; to kill our joy and everything we hold dear on this earth; and to

157

destroy our hopes and visions. He knows he cannot steal away our salvation unto the next age— the Age of Jubilee, that our Father freely gave to us and that we are sealed by professing, *"Jesus Is Lord"*. But he can surely take every other thing that we have or hope to have on earth during this New Covenant Age— unless we are willing to admit that no such thing belongs to us anyway, all these things we claim to own in this age belongs to God. In His *Parable of the Sower* (Mark 4:1-20), Jesus teaches us how to profit on earth by planting the Word firmly in the fertile ground of our heart. In Mark 10:17-22, When the rich man asked Jesus what he could do to inherit eternal life and said that he had kept all the commandments, Jesus told him to sell all of his goods, and give the proceeds to the poor. But the rich man could not agree to such a command— because he had great possessions, and he left Jesus, grieving. Then in verses 23-30 we hear Jesus teaching us that the unwillingness of the rich man to relinquish his possessions was exactly why it is so difficult for such a man to inherit eternal life. But, unlike men who are bound by what they consider to be possible, God does impossible things; and, as He answered Peter, if we are willing to plant His promises in our heart, and surrender to God's perfect will all such things that we hold so dear, we can have an hundredfold return on each of those things we willingly give up. He wants to see if we are willing to act upon our faith in His Word that life here on earth will yield an abundance on every single thing we are willing to give up, no matter how difficult, even impossible it might seem. The seed is the Word (Mark 4:14); as with Abraham, this act of faith will be credited to us as righteousness (Romans 4:3 & 22; Galatians 3:6) — and will abundantly multiply our return.

Our Burden Is Light, Thanks to Christ Jesus

Psalm 51:6-7 offers us the opportunity to have Him search our inward parts. We hear the psalmist David admitting and confessing his sins as he invites the Holy Spirit to search his heart and purge him of evil, *"Behold, You delight in truth in the inward being, and You teach me wisdom in the secret heart. Purge me with hyssop and I shall be clean; wash me and I shall be whiter than snow."* Christ Jesus tells us in Matthew 11:30, *"My yoke is easy, My burden is light."* He paid the cost for our discipleship at Calvary. All we really have to do is commit to discharge the commission Jesus has given to us, serving the Kingdom of God wherever our commission takes us.

We Must Choose Today Which God We Will Serve

Sometimes we think we can lead "two lives" — and just "sit on the fence" concerning our commitment to God's work on earth. That may work for those who want to keep on sojourning and "sneak into Zion" from their deathbed. These "Christian prodigals" need to come home. *City Dwellers* know better. As Joshua's time on earth was nearly over, he charged the people of Israel to choose the God they would serve. We hear him addressing the people in Joshua 24:13-15, saying to them, *"Our God gave you a land on which you had not labored, and cities which you had not built — and you dwell therein; you eat the fruit of vineyards and oliveyards which you did not plant. Now therefore, fear the Lord and serve Him in sincerity and faithfulness; put away the gods which your fathers served beyond the Jordan and in Egypt; or the gods of the Amorites in whose land you dwell — and serve the Lord. And if you are unwilling to serve the Lord, choose this day whom you will serve; but as for me and my house, we will serve the Lord."* We are covenant people. He has made a covenant with us through Christ Jesus our Lord. So, it is up to each one of us to decide today to serve Him.

Have We Made a Covenant with God?

The people's response in Joshua 24 is noteworthy to make the point. They said they recognized what the Lord had done for them; and added, *"He is our God; therefore, we will serve the Lord also"* (Joshua 24:18). They wanted it both ways — to keep their gods, and serve the Lord. Joshua 24:19-28 allows us to hear the discussion that ensues between Joshua and the people. We hear

Joshua's stern voice first, *"That won't do — the Most High God is a jealous God; you have to make a real choice today — and if you choose God, but continue to serve foreign gods, you are turning away from Him — and He will turn away from you and consume you — you won't receive another blessing from God; and even what He has given you He will take away."* "No," the people said, *"we don't want that to happen; we choose to serve God."* Then Joshua said, *"Today then, let you be witnesses against yourselves that you have chosen the Lord, to serve Him."* And they replied, *"We are witnesses,"* and Joshua made covenant with the people on that very day. They made statutes and ordinances to enforce what together as a nation they had agreed to do; and they took a great stone and set it up under the oak in the sanctuary of the Lord. And Joshua said, *"Let this stone be a witness against us, for it has heard all the words of the Lord that He spoke to us, of which we have attested to this day."* And Joshua sent the people away, every man to his inheritance.

So the people chose to serve God only all the days of Joshua — and all the days of the elders who outlived Joshua and had known all the work which the Lord had done for Israel. *City Dwellers*, we cannot have it both ways. The question each of us must ask ourselves, "Have I made this covenant with God?"

"Seek Ye First the Kingdom of God and His Righteousness"

Joshua 24 surely sends a strong message to us today. We note in verse 28 that our inheritance remains intact when we remain in covenant with God. We must choose today whom we will serve, whether the Most High God or other gods— remembering that anything or anyone that becomes a god to us prevents us from enjoying our citizenship in Zion. We need to abandon our old man's habits, perhaps even leave dear old friends— even our own family members may be against us. When God called Jeremiah to be His prophet, He reminded him, *"Even your brothers and the house of your father have dealt treacherously with you; they are in full cry after you. Though they speak fair words to you, believe them not"* (Jeremiah 12:6). We can relate to such interference.

Our Heart Is Always Where Our Treasure Lies

Whatever we think about in our hearts (Proverbs 23:7), we put first in our speech and actions— whatever we truly and earnestly seek after is where our treasure lies. As Jesus teaches us in Matthew 6:21, *"Wherever your treasure lies, there your heart will be also."* We must make difficult choices. We can't fool God. The psalmist David acknowledges his

Creator in Psalm 139:13-17, *"You created my inner being and knit me together in my mother's womb...You know me right well and my frame was not hidden from You; when I was being made in secret, intricately wrought in the depths of the earth, your eyes beheld my uniformed substance and in Your book were written every one of the days that were formed for me, when as yet there were none of them. How precious to me are Your thoughts, O God, and how vast is the sum of them. When I awake I am still with You."* And in verse 23, David asks God to help him with his self-examination, *"Search me, O God, and know my heart. Try me and know my thoughts."*

We Know When We Are
Abiding in the Truth

We know that God loves us so much that He gave us our precious gift of salvation based on our proclaimed faith in God's Word that Jesus is Lord (John 3:16; Romans 10:9). And we know that *"we have passed from death unto life because we love the brethren"* (I John 3:14). We know that we have received the Holy Spirit, and He empowers us to do the work of the Kingdom. These assurances are ours. Far more than that, God knows our thoughts and actions— He knows whether or not we are abiding in Him. I John 3:18-24 addresses this very principle. By examining ourselves and confessing our sins, we know if we are of the truth. Remember who we are in our Father's eyes— *City Dwellers*. The Apostle

John tells us in I John 1:9, *"If we confess our sins, God is faithful and just and will forgive us and cleanse us of all unrighteousness."* Therefore, by confession, we can reassure our hearts before Him when our hearts have condemned us, and be in His presence in Zion the next moment. The Apostle John tells us in I John 3:20-22, *"God is greater than our hearts; and if our hearts do not condemn us, we have confidence before Him — and we receive whatever we ask of Him because we keep His commandments and do what pleases Him."* Just as Joshua and the people agreed to do— we must reaffirm our allegiance to the Most High God daily. We want to spend time with God the Father in Zion everyday— not just some days. *City Dwellers,* we are no longer merely sojourning. God requires our continuous commitment to what ambassadors are required to do. He expects us to be equal to the task, and is waiting for us in His throne room.

Our Flesh Is the Only Reason
We Can't Go to Zion Everyday

We are ready for a closer walk with God because we have accepted the Great Commission He gave us before He left the earth. Jesus does not expect us to discharge this responsibility without spiritual power from on high. Those whom He has chosen to carry on His work on earth are not only entitled to receive the Baptism in the Holy Spirit as a part of their spiritual armor— which

He gives to us, such armament becomes an absolute necessity to defeat the enemy.

We are disciples of Christ Jesus. We are His ambassadors, and we need to be in Zion each and every day, whether we are doing business on great waters or meditating in His Word in our prayer closet. This is the very reason why at the Last Supper when He was still on the earth with us, Jesus prayed the Father for us to be one in Him and to allow Him to be one in us— just as He is one in the Father and the Father is one in Him (John 17:20-22). It's all about oneship— that we may all become perfectly one, that the world may know that the Father sent Jesus into the world to draw men unto Himself; and that we are loved by the Father— for just as He sent Jesus into the world, Jesus sends us— we are one in Him (John 17:25).

Carrying on the work of the Lord on earth should make us realize that some will resist the message of salvation they so desperately need, others will reject the Baptism in the Holy Spirit. But our mission is clear. Jesus established the pattern for us when He sent His disciples into the towns and villages— He armed them with His power and authority (Luke 9 & 10). And Jesus told His disciples to stay in the house or village where they were received, and bless those occupants. We should know that our baptism by fire will require us to sustain assaults on our flesh by the forces of evil that we have never before experienced. But *City Dwellers*, we will overcome evil on earth that accuse and mock us, by the blood of the Lamb and the word of our testimony, as we courageously serve God (Revelation 12:11).

We Should Expect "Troubled Waters" as We Serve God

Psalm 107 tells us what we might expect as we carry out our commission to teach and disciple God's children. It is almost a certainty that we can expect to find troubled waters as we prepare to discharge our responsibility as Christ's ambassadors, and we will need to go to Zion— and spend much time there, receiving strength and instructions on how to carry out our Lord's work on earth. The psalmist writes in verses 23-32, "*Some went down to the sea in ships, doing business on the great waters. They saw the deeds of the Lord, His wondrous works in the deep. For He commanded and raised the stormy wind, which lifted up the waves of the sea. They mounted up to heaven; they went down to the depths...But despite their evil plight, when they cried out to the Lord in their trouble, He delivered them from their distress. He made the storm be still and the waves of the sea were hushed; then they were glad because they had quiet, and God brought them to their desired haven. Let them thank the Lord for His steadfast love, for His wonderful works to the sons of men. Let them extol Him in the congregation of the people, and praise Him in the assembly of the elders.*"

City Dwellers, We Must
Stand Fast to the End

MATTHEW 10:16-17   "Behold, I send you as sheep in the midst of wolves, so be wise as serpents and innocent as doves.   Beware of men — for they will deliver you up to Councils..."

Psalm 107 is great Word, but this message only bolsters our need to be courageous in exercising our ambassadorial responsibilities. When God appointed Joshua to lead the Israelites across the Jordan and into the promised land (Joshua 1:1-3) — God chose Joshua because He needed a man to take the lead who envisioned victory and not defeat; and He told Him in verse 3, *"Every place that the sole of your foot will tread upon I have given to you as I promised to Moses."* God honors His Word.

Numbers 13 offers us an excellent account of Israel's doubt and unbelief that had required them to spend forty years in the wilderness. The people accepted the evil report of ten of twelve spies who returned from a 40-day reconnaissance mission into the land God had given them.   They returned in great fear, testifying that there were giants in the land; and the peoples occupying the land were too strong for Israel to displace; and they should not go in (verses 27-29, 31).

Now forty years later, those same peoples were still there, Moses had died, and all the men who had rendered the evil report had also died—including all the people who had believed them. But both Joshua and Caleb, two of the twelve spies who spied out the Land and who had proven their loyalty and obedience to God at that time were still alive. They had urged the people to then invade the Land immediately—that the Israelites were sufficiently strong to take the promised land, and drive out all the peoples— no matter how great or how many of those peoples came against them.

Joshua Showed Us What One Man Can Do in Obedience to God

It is noteworthy that we hear God assuring Joshua of His presence and help for as long as He lived. *"No man will be able to stand before you all the days of your life. As I was with Moses I will be with you; I will not fail you or forsake you. Be strong and of good courage, for you shall cause this people to inherit the land which I swore to their fathers to give them. Only be strong and very courageous, being careful to do according to all the law which Moses My servant commanded you. Turn not to the right hand or the left so that you may have good success wherever you go. This Book of the Law shall not pass out of your mouth, but you shall meditate on it day and night, that you may be careful to do according to all that is written; for then you shall have good success. Have I not commanded you? Be strong and of good courage; be not frightened or dismayed, for*

the Lord your God is with you wherever you go"
(Joshua 1:5-9).

God knew the magnitude of the task Joshua faced, but knew he was the man to do it. God emphasized the importance of Joshua's staying power. So, God instructed Him to meditate in His Word, the Law, day and night; and three times urged him to be strong and very courageous. He chose the right man. Joshua's baptism by fire had officially begun when he and Caleb demonstrated their courage 40 years before to return the good minority report in the face of their ten brethren— whose evil report had then convinced the people that they could not defeat the inhabitants of the promised land. Even now Joshua remained convinced that the Israelites could take the land, no matter how strong the inhabitants, and that God would be with them. He willingly accepted the responsibility to lead the people into the land. He was the willing vessel God needed.

Joshua's Three Days of Preparation and the Two Spies

After receiving his instructions from God, Joshua decided to take three days of preparation before crossing the Jordan. This valuable time gave him opportunity to meet with his captains and develop a good entry plan needed to take the promised land. One important aspect of the plan included spying out the land— just as Moses had done forty years before. Joshua obviously did not want to repeat the mistakes of the past. The key to the reconnaissance mission would lie in the least possible chance that the enemy would detect the presence of the spies. Forty years before, twelve spies were sent out. When that group of spies returned, ten of the twelve brought back an evil report. He knew God's commandment for him to *"arise, go over this Jordan"* (Joshua 1:2) called for quick action. So, instead of repeating what had happened 40 years before, Joshua used only two spies to view the land instead of twelve, and it took them but three days instead of forty. He had perfect divine guidance. When these two spies returned in three days, the report was quite different from the one given by ten of twelve spies who spent 40 days searching out the land forty years earlier. So Joshua decided on two spies and sent them out. Hidden by Rahab, when they returned, these spies reported to Joshua that they should take the land immediately, saying, *"Truly the Lord has given all the land into our hands; and moreover, all the inhabitants of the land are fainthearted because of us."*

Blessed Assurance, Jesus Is Ours.

Joshua's assurance from the Most High God that He would always be with Him is essentially the same assurance that Christ Jesus gave us when we were appointed as His ambassadors to the nations before He ascended to Zion following His crucifixion and resurrection. Matthew 28:20 is part of the Great Commission, as we hear Christ Jesus saying, *"I am with you always, even until the end of the age."* The Apostle Paul also gives us the same assurance in Romans 8:31, *"If God is for us, who can be against us."*

We Stand on the Truth of the Word

These scriptures (Matthew 28:20; Romans 8:31) confirm the ever-abiding presence of the Spirit of the Most High God and our Lord Jesus. God is not mocked (Galatians 6:7). He desires to empower you so that you may give Him the glory (First Corinthians 10:31). *"All things are possible to him who believes"* (Mark 9:23). At the *Last Supper* Jesus promised to send us the Holy Spirit, saying, *"If a man loves Me, he will keep My Word, and My Father will love Him, and We will come to him and make Our home with him"* (John 14:23). Sometimes our disbelieving fellow Christians will join in the mockery the devil throws at us, telling us that the things we hope for are impossible. "All that has passed away," they may say to you. Don't believe it. We know better. Just stand. No matter what the circumstances, stand on His promises. Jesus said, *"They will hate you for My Name's sake, but he who stands to the end will be saved. When they persecute you in one town, flee to another; for truly I say to you, you will not have gone through all the towns of Israel before the Son of Man comes"* (Matthew 10:22-23).

God's Ways Are Not Our Ways, Sometimes Fewer Is Better

Isaiah 55:8 tells us, God's ways are not our ways. God searches for just one willing vessel who will listen to His voice, without fear of the enemy, no matter how daunting the challenge appears to be. God has the battle plan. Why not ask Him to discuss it with us? Ask, seek, and knock (Matthew 7:7).

When we think about defeating the enemy in battle, we immediately believe that the larger our army, the better our odds of winning. We seem to always want to assume things that are not in evidence. Our flesh is easily led to believe only what the world says is true. And the world always assumes the obvious. So, we rely on the numbers game, "playing the odds" — more must be better, bigger will defeat little. Not always. Sometimes less is better. Small contingents usually can more easily agree to rely upon cardinal principles that lead to victory rather than defeat. Sometimes all God needs is one willing vessel, to partner with Him.

Gideon and His 300 Men

Another obedient man was Gideon. Long after the Israelites had taken the promised land, they

him. Refusing to put on standard battle armor; David took with him his staff, a sling and five stones. And while Goliath was scoffing at the presence of David, who had dared to face him, David said to Goliath in verses 45-46, *"You come to me with a sword and a spear, with a shield, but I come to thee in the Name of the Lord of hosts, the God of the armies of Israel, whom you have defied. This day will the Lord deliver you into my hand; and I will smite you and take your head from you."* We know the rest of the story — it took one stone for God's plan to prevail. The Philistines fled when their warrior was slain — the battle was over. One unlikely hero was able to do this because He did it in the Name of the Lord of hosts. And David believed his God would deliver Goliath into his hand; and God received the glory while he gave David the victory on earth.

We Have Victory Over Death

One man, our Lord Jesus, gave His life to defeat death at Calvary to ensure that we can defeat death also. He does not require that we give up ours to death. There were other Christian martyrs in the early church, but today Jesus simply requires us to die to self. When we do this, we are ready to *Mount Up to Zion*. Jesus desires that we dwell with Him in Zion. This means that we must focus on things of the Spirit and not the flesh. Hebrews 12:1-2 teaches us to lay aside any weight that causes us to sin; and to fix our eyes on Christ Jesus, the Pioneer and Perfecter of our faith. The Apostle Paul's letter to the Galatians puts this lesson in perspective for us: *"Those who belong to Christ Jesus have crucified the flesh with its passions and desires"* (Gal. 5:24). Our surrender must be a willful act.

7

The Weapons of Our Warfare

MATTHEW 3:11 John the Baptist said to the people, "I baptize you with water for repentance, but the One Who is coming after me is mightier than I, whose sandals I am not worthy to carry; He will baptize you with the Holy Spirit and with fire.

II Corinthians 10:4. The weapons of our warfare are not worldly, but spiritual with divine power to destroy the strongholds of evil.

It would have been impossible for any person present on the day Jesus was baptized in the River Jordan to know or understand the enormity of what was taking place. It was a water baptismal service administered by John the Baptist for all whom he baptized to repent of their sins. So, when Jesus presented himself for baptism, everyone else but John himself saw it as nothing out of the ordinary. John recognized the Messiah, and would have prevented Jesus from receiving this baptism, knowing that Jesus had no cause or reason to repent— that he was the one whom should be baptized by Jesus. But Jesus told John that such was required, so John baptized Him in the River Jordan together with many others.

When Jesus came out of the water, no one, not even John the Baptist, saw the Holy Spirit descending upon and alighting on Jesus or heard the voice of God the Father expressing His pleasure with Jesus. Because no one except Jesus could have seen or heard things occurring in the Spirit, using spiritual senses. Jesus was God the Father's Anointed Chosen One. No one other than Jesus would be blessed with such a powerful anointing until the Day of Pentecost after the New Covenant took effect at Calvary — 40 days following Jesus' ascension — when 120 of His disciples — including the eleven, His mother and brothers, would be chosen by Jesus to receive a portion of His anointing (Acts 1:12-14). That day marked the beginning of the new man in Christ (II Corinthians 5:17).

We Need to Bind Up Carnal Things

While it is physically impossible to bind up imaginations and fantasies; the evil desires of our physical eyes; the cares of this world; evil thoughts and actions; careless words — and any other carnal thing, all of which are contrary to the perfect will of God, our spirit man empowered by the Holy Spirit knows better. He can and will bind up all such carnal things in obedience to Christ Jesus. This is why the Baptism in the Holy Spirit is so important. With this baptism, we are enabled to become the new creation in Christ Jesus; and empowered to overcome evil. The Apostle Paul said it right,

"We are a new creation; the old has passed away *and the new has come"* (II Corinthians 5:17).

Jesus Sent the Holy Spirit
His Resurrection and Ascension

The significance of the Holy Spirit's arrival on earth cannot be overstated. John 14:15-17 and Acts 1:8 tell us much about how and why we have the Holy Spirit in us today. At the Last Supper before His arrest, Jesus gave His disciples a charge with a promise, *"If you love Me, you will keep My commandments. And I will pray the Father, and He will give you another Counselor, to be with you forever, even the Spirit of Truth, Whom the world cannot receive, because it neither sees Him nor knows Him; you know Him, for He dwells with you now and will be in you."*

From that Day of Pentecost when Jesus baptized 120 in the Holy Spirit until now, the Holy Spirit has been with all Christians who profess, *"Jesus Is Lord"*. It is truly up to each one of us whether or not we will allow Jesus to baptize us in the Holy Spirit, so that He will alight upon us, come into our hearts and infill us as He did Jesus (Matthew 3:16). Every believer must decide. If we truly believe that all things are possible with God, we will decide to let Him in; we will be able to "go up" to Zion; and there Jesus will surely arm all of His disciples with His anointed power and authority.

The Full Infilling of the Holy Spirit
Is the Baptism

The full infilling of the Holy Spirit means our flesh no longer controls us. Jesus instructs us in John 12:24, *"Unless a kernel of wheat dies and falls to the ground, it remains a single seed. But if it dies it produces many seeds."* There is so much work for us to do as Christ's ambassadors. He wants more ambassadors. Unless we can be His vessel to gather the harvest and bring in the sheaves, we may as well wait until our final breath on earth to go to Zion— only to claim salvation for ourselves. Christ Jesus wants us with Him in Zion now so he can commission us to discharge specific assignments for Him, and send us back and forth from Zion to Jerusalem— to proclaim the good news of the gospel of Christ Jesus wherever and whenever we have opportunity to do so. We are the New Covenant Generation of *City Dwellers.* This requires us to be fully infilled and fully empowered with His Spirit.

Making Preparations for Battle

Yes, we can *Mount Up to Zion.* We may be sojourning on earth for a brief time, but we know that our spirit man is not bound by our flesh. We are indeed the soldiers of Jesus Christ; and, as such, we should be ready for a confrontation with the enemy at any given moment. We know that he is clever and will attack any part of our flesh, mind and soul. He knows better than to attack our spirit man— our spirit man knows that satan has been defeated. But our flesh and mind are vulnerable. So, armed with the power and authority of the anointing that the Baptism in the Holy Spirit gives us, we prepare for battle with our enemy.

First, we need to *Mount Up to Zion* to renew our strength, discuss the battle plan with the Father and Christ Jesus, and put on our armor. However, before we can mount up, we must cast off the works of darkness and remove our filthy garments; and, with a clean turban on our head and dressed in clean apparel, we invite the Holy Spirit to take us up to Zion. In the Spirit, we *Mount up to Zion* where Jesus meets us on the highway, takes us through the city gates and opens the door to our Father's throne room.

There we go from our limited strength to God's omnipotent strength (Psalm 84:7). And, in the presence of both the Father and Christ Jesus, we discuss the battle plan, intercede for our brethren, present our petitions, and converse with them concerning any special assignment they desire us to undertake and receive special instructions. Jesus tells us in John 10:9 that we come out again and find pasture in Jerusalem, that is, our own little Jerusalem where God wants us to be.

Jesus Baptizes Us With Fire to
Ensure That We Are Able to Stand

John the Baptist baptized with water as an outward sign of a believer's cleansing of sin and his repentance. But in Matthew 3:11, he told the people, *"I baptize you with water for repentance, but He Who is coming after me is mightier than I, Whose sandals I am not worthy to carry; He will baptize you in the Holy spirit and with fire."* With the Baptism in the Holy Spirit comes the anointing of power and authority we need to defeat satan on earth— in the spiritual realm. Jesus knows that we will need His strength for the battle against satan that is certain to come after we have received the Baptism in the Holy Spirit. However, if the bugle gives an indistinct sound, who will get ready for battle (I Corinthians 14:8). So, Jesus must give all His disciples the baptism by fire. The demonic forces of the world realize that fully infilled Christians are strong spiritual enemies; and we can surely expect the devil to attack us in an attempt to get us back to our flesh and out of his way. Until we have received the Baptism in the Holy Spirit we have no defenses.

No, satan cannot deprive us of our helmet of salvation (Ephesians 6:17), but why would we dare face him in battle without arraying ourselves in the full armor of God (Ephesians 6:10-18), allowing him to inflict many grievous wounds so he can easily control our dominion and keep us in a constant state of defeat? Now that we have the Baptism we will be able to stand against the powers of death in the world that always attack our own flesh. This is a much lesser degree of the same baptism by fire Jesus went through in His wilderness ordeal, even unto the very night of His arrest in the Garden of Gethsemane (Matthew 4:1-11 & 26:47-57). But because He had to endure his trials and tribulations, we must do so also— so that we, too, can be trusted to resist the devil's temptations and assaults on our flesh. This is what Jesus meant in Luke 14:27 when He said to us, *"Whosoever does not carry his own cross and come after Me cannot be My disciple.*

Our Lord Jesus Helps Us to
Put on the Full Armor of God

The full armor of God (Ephesians 6:11-18) is available to us only in Zion— where we are married to Jesus. We go up to Zion to receive strength for the battle from our Husband. Zion is where King Jesus equips us with His armor of light so that we can walk in the light of His countenance as we participate in the joyous festal shout, inviting the Lord's presence (Psalm 89:15). Paul tells us in Romans 13:12 that when we put on our Husband's armor, we put on our Lord Jesus Himself who is the Light—and we thereby forsake the devil, casting off the works of darkness which have invaded our flesh.

We Can Claim the High Ground
on the Battlefield

Thank God the Baptism in the Holy Spirit is available to all believers; and with it the anointing of Christ Jesus that we may go up to Zion and receive the strength we need to go through such a baptism of fire. Moses faced the enemy many times in his confrontations with Pharaoh when he needed God's rod of power and authority. But the mind of Moses — as strong as it was for an Old Covenant man of great faith, equipped with the rod of power, fell into fear. We understand how it happens — even to spirit-empowered children of God.

It is so easy for us to second-guess Moses. Maybe he should have said to the people, "Go forward now in the name of Our God. I will stretch out my hand with the rod of God's authority that He gave me, and He will lead us across this sea. Our God will deliver us today, and you will see these Egyptians no more." But how often do we say to ourselves when we realize too late, "I missed it — I didn't hear the sound of the bugle. I should have bound that up; I should have said that; I should have done that." Why was Moses not able to give this command without God's prompting? Because he was an Old Covenant man and had no savior in Christ Jesus — he was unable to put on the mind of Christ (I Corinthians 2:16). Moses was unable to go up to Zion to gain the strength he needed for the battle. But we can. When we are

New Covenant sons and daughters of God. When we receive the Baptism in the Holy Spirit, we have God's rod of power. We have the presence and the empowerment of the Holy Spirit, our ever-present help in time of need — trouble and decision (Psalm 46:1-3).

Thank God that in the throne room we New Covenant believers can be strengthened and made ready to *"Go forward"* into a battle against an enemy that would otherwise surely defeat us. When we sing a familiar old hymn, we realize we are soldiers of our Lord Jesus whom He is preparing to do His bidding on earth — *Onward Christian Soldiers, marching as to war.* As we march to victory on earth, we proclaim, *"Jesus Is Lord".* And because we love our Lord Jesus the Father promises us, *"If a man loves Me, he will keep My words in his heart, and My Father will love him, and We will come to him and make Our home with him"* (John 14:23).

God Intends for Jerusalem on Earth to Be Like Zion in Heaven

For some of us, the process of receiving the Baptism in the Holy Spirit is almost instantaneous; others of us may require years of nurture. More importantly, we understand that as we receive this Baptism God intends for Jerusalem on earth to be like Zion in heaven. And Jesus is depending upon committed and empowered Spirit-filled believers to see this mission accomplished. This is the purpose of the Great Commission. It is very important we understand how we are changed by the Baptism. We will be empowered to use spiritual senses not available to us before, the immediate evidence of which is our ability to speak in tongues.

Thus begins the transition from our virtually complete reliance on our physical senses, to new domains of knowledge. Seeing, hearing, tasting, touching, smelling— and distinguishing good from evil take on a completely new meaning. We experience a strong sense of perception that what we can now do in the Spirit is magnanimous compared to what "surface" abilities we exercise in the flesh. We become almost instantly aware of the severe physical limitations of our mind and soul to even hear the Word of God much less to be able to apply it to our own circumstances. Of course we will use our physical senses for certain daily needs and functions, but no longer should we rely on them to establish our kingship and lordship for Christ Jesus. Admittedly, in no way will our flesh ever be able to defeat satan. But in the Spirit Jesus defeated him soundly at Calvary, taking back from him all the power and authority in the earth that Adam gave up. In the Spirit we will reign victorious over him and his demons. Only after we complete this transition from our salvation status to one of full service for the Master, equipped with the full armor of God, will we be ready to discharge our commission from Christ Jesus (Matthew 28:18-20). We have an arsenal of weapons we can use against evil, including the whole armor of God with the ability to pray in a language that demons cannot understand. But we must remember one more: perseverance. When we have utilized all the keys to victory that we know to use, including praying constantly in our prayer language; have sought after other keys to victory in Zion; and have knocked on the door of the throne room to get a new supply of our Father's strength, we just stand.

The Baptism of Fire Tests Us
under Combat Conditions

Jesus baptizes Spirit-filled believers with fire to ensure that we have been tested under fire. Believers who have been baptized in the Holy Spirit and are operating in the anointing are a hindrance to satan and he wants us out of his way. Jesus knows this attack is coming so He makes sure that we are battle-tested and able to stand under actual combat conditions. And where will this battle take place? In our own mind. We must put our contaminated old man to death. And with his death, we also cast down doubts and fears, imaginations and arguments, and any other stronghold that rises up against the perfect will of God; and attempts to interfere with us walking in the Way and the Truth, and serving His Kingdom on earth (II Cor. 10:5). When we have done this, we should not be concerned for the outcome. Hebrews 12:27-29 tells us that our God is a *"consuming fire"* who will remove all things about us that can be shaken out.

The writer of the Book of Hebrews charges us to let God burn away all the chaff in our lives, saying to us in verses 28-29, *"Therefore let us be grateful for receiving a Kingdom that cannot be shaken, and thus let us offer to God acceptable worship, with reverence and awe, for our God is a consuming fire."* This is a confirmation of what John the Baptist preached in Luke 3:16-17, saying, *"I baptize you with water, but He Who is mightier than I is coming, the thong of whose sandals I am not worthy to untie; He will baptize you with the Holy Spirit and with fire. His winnowing fork is in His hand, to clear His threshing floor, and to gather the fruit into His granary, but the chaff He will burn with unquenchable fire."*

Transitioning from the
Old Man to the New Man in Christ

The Apostle Paul reminds all believers in First Corinthians 10:12, *He who thinks that he is standing had best beware lest he will surely fall.* So I make this declaration concerning some of you who are reading this book to prepare for a celebration of your approaching victory over your own flesh. To you I say this: your celebration will begin when you truly see in the Spirit that you are transitioning from the carnal lifestyle of your old man, which is the Old Covenant, to a Holy Spirit led, spirit man-controlled life. And when you know that you have invited the presence of God into your life, the Holy Spirit will move in you; and you will begin to hear the joyful sound of the festal shout (Psalm 89:15). And you will only need to open your mouth and start speaking to realize you are speaking in a tongue that only God recognizes. When this spiritual experience produces these things on earth we realize that only the Holy Spirit can make that happen for us— and He so wants that very outcome for us.

The Festal Shout Is Our Call to Battle

Going up to Zion before we take our last breath is a precious higher gift Christ Jesus has made available for us. There can be no doubt that Jesus wants us there now. He's offered us a marriage proposal— to reside with Him in Beulah Land; and it could not possibly help the Kingdom of God if we waited until after our life in this age ends to accept His proposal. No matter how hard we strive or how many hours we toil, the power and might of our flesh will fail us when we are up against the forces of evil. That position is where satan wants us. But in the Spirit and in Zion, Jesus has already defeated him. We cannot marry Jesus on earth no matter how "spiritual" we may think we are, because Jesus resides in Zion. We must "mount up" and "go up" to marry him.

Study the Word closely. Jesus would not have told us that we will go in and come out, and find pasture (John 10:9) if we would not be spending a lot of time there. We will be doing a lot of traveling. Jesus would not have prayed the Father that He wanted his disciples *"with Me where I am"* (John 17:24) if that did not mean now in this age. And for the eleven and others in the early church, these travels were to begin soon after the Day of Pentecost following His ascension. Jesus would not be required to wait long.

While the Holy Spirit resides with all Christians, until we experience the Baptism in the Holy Spirit we do not have His anointing within us. This is very important. Our case in point is what happened when Jesus himself received this baptism after John the Baptist had baptized Him with water at the River Jordan. Jesus went up immediately from the Jordan and saw the Holy Spirit descending and alighting upon Him, and heard His Father's voice of approval (Matthew 3:16-17). The very next verse (Matthew 4:1) tells us that Jesus was led up by the Holy Spirit into the wilderness to be tempted by the devil.

When We Pass Through the Fire
We Become Equally Yoked

Isaiah 62:4 confirms our New Covenant with God. Beulah Land— the land all about God's Holy Mount Zion, was not available to Old Covenant people. They could not be married to God because God could not be equally yoked with a sinful generation, convicted and condemned by the Law. They had no perfect sacrifice to cleanse them from sin; therefore their land was forever a forsaken land, unable to produce and yield fruit acceptable to God. He had no delight in them; thus God separated Himself from them.

But in Isaiah 62:4 the prophet Isaiah is prophesying about the relationship that exists today between our Bridegroom, Christ Jesus, and the assembly of saints whose spirits are on earth today. We are invisible to the natural man and to the physical senses of the world, but clearly visible to the Spirit of God the Father and the Son, and to each other— spirit to spirit. We are the invisible church. Our bodies, souls, spirits, and everything we own— especially our land, are married to God. Our marriage covenant guarantees us the right to live with Christ Jesus, our Husband— where He lives, just as Jesus prayed the Father at the Last Supper for us to be where He is (John 17:24). Our husband lives in Zion. And His Spirit and the Father's Spirit dwell within us (John 14:23).

Psalm 48:12-13 invites us to walk about Zion, go round about her, number her towers, consider well her ramparts, go through her citadels; that we may tell our children and grandchildren that this is God—our God forever. And Jesus will be our guide. This is not a hard thing. The Holy Spirit will carry us up to Zion; Jesus will meet us on the highway for the redeemed (Isaiah 35:8-10); and take us on a tour of His garden, the Holy City and the Father's Holy Mount Zion.

A Baptism That Lets Us Know We Are City Dwellers

What does the Baptism in the Holy Spirit mean for us? When Jesus was baptized by John the Baptist in the River Jordan, everyone present saw it happen— with their natural eyes, i.e., with their physical sense of sight. For this reason, Jesus told John the Baptist that His water baptism was necessary to fulfill all righteousness. The people believed that the water cleansed a person from unrighteousness— and the water baptism was an outward sign of their purification— and Jesus in the flesh was one of them. When Jesus received the Baptism in the Holy Spirit, His spiritual senses were immediately enabled. And He was instantly empowered. Jesus went up immediately from the water. He could now see clearly in the Spirit— with spiritual eyes. Only

Jesus saw the heavens opened and the Spirit of God descending and alighting on Him.

At the Moment We First Believed

I JOHN 1:5-7 ...God is light and in Him is no darkness at all...If we walk in the light, as He is in the light, we have fellowship with one another, and the blood of Jesus cleanses us from sin.

Our God is an amazing God. He wants so much for each one of us to live in divine prosperity, beginning now — to return home. God allowed us to see the light before we knew the magnitude of what we had seen. The light we see now is blindness to our natural eyes, and will never be understood by the world. But it is the light of the anointing of Christ Jesus that shines out of darkness. When we truly receive Christ Jesus into our hearts and make Him the Lord of our life, we begin life anew, living in Him and walking in His footsteps (Col. 2:6).

Under the Old Covenant — before Calvary and the Day of Pentecost when the empowerment of 120 of the saints by the Holy Spirit occurred, the light of God's glory and presence could not be seen in the Spirit because the Holy Spirit was not on earth. Therefore, God had to appear to the people so their physical eyes could behold His presence — this was the only light they had. Thus the light of His presence was never seen with natural eyes unless God allowed it. This occurred rarely.

Psalm 89:15 refers to it as the festal shout because of the sheer joyful sound of such an occasion. Numbers 6:24-26 records the Aaronic Benediction God then gave the people— used by Christians and Jews today to invite the Lord's presence, *"The Lord bless you and keep you; the Lord make His face to shine upon you and be gracious unto you; The Lord lift up His countenance upon you and give you peace."*

God gave Christ Jesus to whosoever in the world believes in Him (John 3:16). That means all of us— indiscriminately. We whosoevers are the anyones the Apostle Peter refers to in Acts 10:35 *"In every nation anyone who fears God and does works of righteousness is acceptable to Him."* We anyones are all called, and, from our midst, any and all of us are chosen— it's really left up to us. Jesus has offered us a marriage proposal. To say, "Yes", is one thing— to accept and live by the marriage vows is another.

Just as it takes faith for a marriage to prosper, it takes faith to believe God. This is why Abraham is called the "Father of Our Faith"— i.e., the Father of all of us who believe God without circumcision of the body (Romans 4:11). And because God shows no favoritism— not even to any one of the anyones, every man has been given the measure of faith God has assigned to him (Romans 12:3). What we do with the measure God has given us determines whether or not we will be given more— or if what we have been given will be taken away from us (Matthew 25:14-30). When God called Abraham, He told him, *"Go to the land I will show you. And I will make of you A great nation…I will bless those who bless you, and him who curses you I will curse; and by you all the families of the earth shall bless themselves"* (Genesis 12:1-3).

So Abraham went; and as we read in Genesis 15:2-6, God promised him an heir (Isaac), though his wife Sarah was barren. Nonetheless, God told him to try to count the stars in the heavens— that his descendants through Isaac would be just as numerous as the stars; and Abraham believed God, and his faith in God's promise was reckoned (credited) to him as righteousness. And this prophecy by God Himself blesses us today. Men and women of faith are the sons and daughters of Abraham (Galatians 3:6-7). As the Apostle Paul teaches us, Now the promises were made to Abraham and his spiritual offspring, which is Christ— and not to his physical offsprings (Galatians 3:16-17). As we read in Genesis 17:6 and 16, God promised Abraham, *"I will make nations of you, and kings shall come forth from you…I will bless Sarah, and give you a son by her; she will be a mother of nations and kings of the peoples shall come from her."*

The Persistency of a
Believer's Faith Reaps Rewards

To see the effect of this covenant for all believers, read Matthew 15:21-28 for the account of the Canaanite woman Jesus encountered on his way to Tyre and Sidon. She came to Jesus pleading with him to heal her daughter who was possessed by a demon. His disciples begged Him to send her away, and Jesus finally answered her, saying, *"It is not fair to take the children's bread and throw it to the dogs."* But she would not go, saying to Jesus, *"Yes, Lord, but even the dogs eat the crumbs that fall from the master's table."* She believed. Then Jesus answered her, *"O woman, great is your faith. Be it done for you as you desire."* And her daughter was healed instantly. Jesus honored the faith of those who believed in Him— regardless of race, color, or nationality. Even from the time of the exodus of the Jews from Egypt when 600,000 men of Israel, not counting women and children, despoiled the Egyptians and departed the land, a mixed multitude went with them (Ex. 12:35-38). Surely today most of us who are not Jews by bloodline would be called part of the mixed multitude; and, by faith, are members of the household of God.

A Roman Centurion's Faith

On yet another occasion concerning a gentile, Luke 7:1-10 records that one day as Jesus entered the city of Capernaum, a Roman centurion who had a sick slave at the point of death sent elders of the Jews to ask Jesus to come heal his slave. They vouched for the centurion, telling Jesus that the centurion loved the Jewish nation and had built them a synagogue. But as Jesus was on his way there, the centurion sent friends out to tell Jesus that he was not even worthy to have Jesus come under his roof; but that he was a man under authority, and if Jesus would just say the word he knew his slave would be healed. Jesus remarked that not even in Israel had he found such faith, and the slave was healed.

A Child Cannot Retract His Heritage

What about children? Will they also receive God's blessings? Yes. Children are innocent until they become of an age to reason things out for themselves and make their own choices. When His disciples asked Jesus in Matthew 18:1-4, *"Which one of us is the greatest in the Kingdom of Heaven? Jesus replied with a child in his arms, "Unless you turn and become like children you will never enter the Kingdom. Whosoever humbles himself like this child is the greatest in the Kingdom of Heaven. "* Here again is a case of a whosoever. God just does not play favorites. When we think too much of ourselves, our flesh is showing. A child cannot retract his heritage. He did not ask to come into the world. It matters not the child's bloodline to God. The innocent will be blessed.

We Are Whosoevers,
One Nation and We Can Go Up to Zion

With these accounts as reference points, First Peter 2:5-9 helps us to see and hear God speaking to all of us whose hearts are right toward Him. We are the whosoevers, living stones, a chosen generation and a holy nation. The entire New Covenant Generation is chosen and blessed — as one holy people who believe in one God; one generation, one faith that proclaims, *"Jesus is Lord"*; one powerful baptism; one body of believers; one royal priesthood; one Kingdom of God in which we serve as kings and priests under the authority of King Jesus Christ; and all the nations of Abraham are one family of blessed believers, obedient to God and trusting in His Word. We are among them.

God Shows Partiality —
to Whosoevers and Anyones

What does it mean to us and to God when we declare ourselves to be God's chosen few? Does it mean that other Christians are not among us — and that somehow God is favoring a select few of us? I Peter 2:9 teaches us, *we are a chosen generation, a holy nation, God's Own people.* But before we discuss the chosen generation, we should ask ourselves, "Who incurs God's favor? " God does not play favorites, so we are not the only blessed ones. But we are among the blessed whosoevers, the blessed anyones.

All Anyones in the World
Are Favored Today.

God does not draw any distinction among us anyones either. He favors all of us; whereas the entire Old Covenant Generation fell into His disfavor due to their unbelief in His Word, ultimately rejecting Jesus as Lord, and proving their inability to keep God's commandments. No matter how great the works of our forefathers, the entire generation remained in his disfavor until Jesus forgave them as He was dying on the cross (Luke 23:34). Remember: the Israelites' acceptance of the evil majority report from the spies who went out to search out the promised land prevented all of God's people from entering the promised land and required the entire nation to wander in the wilderness for another forty years— including the loyal minority (Numbers 13:1-34).

Acts 10:34-35 answers any and every ignorant query asked by "a works only" Christian. And Peter said to them, *"God shows no partiality, but in every nation anyone who fears Him and does works of righteousness is acceptable to Him."* God still sees His people in captivity, and He needs us to "unshackle our own brethren", and release them from captivity in this life. Just as God commissioned Moses in Exodus 3:7-10, Jesus has likewise commissioned each of us, saying, *"I have seen the affliction of My people in Egypt, have heard their cries, and know their sufferings. My Father sent Me into the world to give up My life— that you may live in Me and carry out the*

199

work I laid as the cornerstone; and that you may deliver My people from the evil and sorrow of this world. And you, My child, are My man from Zion to bring them up out of that land to a good and broad land, a land flowing with milk and honey."

We know that God desires for all His children to prosper— Jesus is courting all whosoevers, i.e., all of us who believe Jesus is Lord and are saved by the blood He shed for us at Calvary. Many are innocent children in need of a shepherd. We have work to do on their behalf. Many have slept too long, not hearing Jesus knocking on the door and calling their names; some have put off their garments, don't know how to put them back on, and have become sick in their sinful ways; some have heard Jesus calling but failed to answer— missing opportunities, only later seeking Him but finding Him not; some have fallen into dungeons of evil and are crying out for help; and others have been beaten down by watchmen who have pounced upon them and condemned their every misdeed (Song of Solomon 5:2-7; Psalm 107:4, 10, 17).

"Works Only" Christians Will Enter the Kingdom— But Why Not Now?

Whatever the case, God wants His Own to come home. But how will they get home if they can't find their way? They may desire to come, but, like the prodigal son, are too ashamed. It's not the man himself who incurs the favor or disfavor of

God the Father. He loves us all— all of us are made in God's image, after His likeness…male and female He created all of us (Genesis 1:26-27).

God loved each of us so much when He made us that He intended our image to be the same as His and His Son Jesus. It doesn't make sense that He would show some of us favor and others disfavor. Christians will never enter the Kingdom of Heaven by their "works only". II Chronicles 16:9 tells us, *The eyes of the Lord run to and fro throughout the whole earth to show his might on behalf of those whose heart is blameless toward him.* A man's earthly works, i.e., all of his good deeds, will never be credited to him as righteousness. But his works of faith will produce results. When a man plants the Word of God in the fertile field of His heart, and believes that he will receive what he hopes and asks for, without doubting, he will (Mark 11:22-23).

It is the intent of a man's heart and the fruit he produces thereof that matter to God— not His works. These are our true brethren. Jesus commissioned us all as "fetchers"— as fishers of men, to bring His precious lambs home (John 21:15-17).

Revisiting the story of Cain and Able helps us to further understand the question of God's impartiality. As we read in Genesis 4:4-5, *"God had regard for Abel and his offering, but for Cain and his offering He had no regard."* Why so? Was God showing partiality toward Abel over Cain because Abel's offering was a lamb and Cain's the fruit of the ground? No. Remember that Abel kept sheep and therefore had sheep to give God; Cain was a tiller of the ground; and therefore had the fruit of the ground to give God. It was the intent of Cain's heart that made him give an offering of fruit to God while out of Abel's heart came the very best he could give to God— the firstlings of his flock. God gives us His very best— can we not give Him ours?

So it is that which is in a man's heart that produces his good or bad spiritual fruit. Proverbs 23:7 tells us, *As a man thinketh in his heart, so he is.* The Apostle Paul tells us in I Cor. 2:14—3:3, the natural man cannot think spiritually and therefore cannot receive the gifts of the Spirit because they are folly to him, and he is not able to understand them; the carnal man thinks about the desires of his own flesh, and must be milk-fed; but the spiritual man has the mind of the anointing of Christ Jesus. Many of our brethren need reprogramming, to think on things of the Spirit and to rethink what life is about.

We Are "Peter"— And Jesus Gave Us the Keys to the Kingdom

MATTHEW 16:18 "And I say unto you, you are Peter, and upon this rock I will build My church.

And the powers of death shall not prevail against it."

Not only are we the chosen generation, Jesus also calls us who answer the call, "Peter", based on Peter's profession in Matthew 16:15-19, when Peter was asked by Jesus, *"Who do you say I am?" Peter replied, "You are the Christ — the Son of the Living God."* And Jesus answered him, *"Blessed are you, Simon Bar-Jona."* Notice that Jesus calls him by his birth name. When He uses the name, Peter, in verse 18, Jesus is referring not only to his rock-solid faith, but symbolically to the faith all of us chosen ones have in God's Word. For Jesus goes on to say this to Peter: *"For flesh and blood did not reveal this to you, but My Father Who is in heaven. And I tell you, you are Peter, and on this rock I will build My church, and the powers of death shall not prevail against it. I will give you the keys of the Kingdom of Heaven, and whatever you bind on earth shall be bound in heaven, and whatever you loose on earth shall be loosed in heaven."*

What Are the Keys to Heaven Worth to Us?

Jesus is saying that we can have the keys to the Kingdom of God — He will give us these keys. Jesus is saying that the Holy Spirit will reveal the principles of prosperity to us, and give us wisdom and understanding to have the abundant life here on earth — to decide things by declaring them done, and thereby binding or loosing those things which are in heaven. But He needs us in Zion with Him now so He can commission us to bring His children home.

Is Our Salvation Complete?

Yes, our salvation is a complete gift. God is not an incomplete God. However, by not deciding the blessed life Jesus offers us now means we reject the abundant life now. This means but one thing: these reluctant brethren, believers without a commitment— sunny day Christians, have chosen to continue living under the Old Covenant spiritually just as did the people of that generation who also rejected the call by their continued unbelief in God's Word and disobedience to His commandments— so often losing their special favor with God and grieving Him terribly. God had told Moses and the Israelites many times that He would show them their homeland— a land flowing with milk and honey (Exodus 3:8); even at the time just before the spies were sent out when He instructed Moses, *"Send men to spy out the land of Canaan, which I give to the people of Israel; from each tribe of their fathers shall you send a man, every one a leader among them (Numbers 13:1)."* However, a doubting people chose the evil majority report— and paid dearly. The Israelites spent forty more years in the wilderness.

The Abundant Life Is a Blessing for Today

Some ardent believers may find comfort in knowing that their salvation remains intact for the hereafter, but remain "unblessed" today. And their absence at the marriage feast in Zion means one thing— while their salvation is complete, their blessings are incomplete— waiting to be claimed in Zion. While they are secured for eternity, their refusal of Jesus' proposal of marriage now may relegate them to years in the wilderness, denying them the abundant life in divine prosperity only Jesus can offer on earth— the life God the Father sent Jesus to earth in the flesh for all whosoevers and anybodies to have and for which He died.

We Are God's Children— Chosen to Glorify Him

Matthew 1:1 The book of the genealogy of Jesus Christ, the son of David, the son of Abraham.

When Jesus came to earth in the flesh, everything changed. In His first sermon after His Own Baptism in the Holy Spirit and spending forty days in the wilderness, He healed and blessed us, and empowered us to walk in the light of His countenance. Our Lord Jesus showed us how to pray, taught us the principle of using our gift of faith and the principles of righteous living; and explained to us the secrets of declaring, sowing and reaping, binding and loosing. He declared the purpose for His coming— to give us the abundant life in this life and in the age to come, and told us that He is the door to the throne room. He exposed evil wherever He found it.

At the Last Supper He sanctified us in the truth, told us that He was going to prepare a place for us in Zion so that we could be where He is; made us joint heirs with Him of the Kingdom of God; declared our kingdom to be in Him, and promised to send us the Holy Spirit to live in us. He established His Kingdom as one of the Spirit, declaring it so during His public trial before Pilate. And, with the shedding of His blood, He empowered us to have our sins forgiven by our confession and profession of faith in Him as our Lord and Savior. While dying on the cross, He completed the Old Covenant and established the New Covenant with us— becoming our High Priest and making us a royal priesthood under His authority; and giving us access to God the Father— even into the Holy of Holies.

Before Jesus ascended, He commissioned us to go into all nations and baptize them, following the guidelines He established when He sent His disciples into the towns and villages. This is our charge to serve the Kingdom; and this we will do— unless we decide to remain prodigals— refusing to believe that His blood cleansed us of all unrighteousness.

When We Became a New Man in Christ
We Changed Our Dwelling Place

When we dwell in Zion and see beautiful Beulah Land (Isaiah 30:19), we know we are only here on earth in our body of flesh as visitors. When we truly became a new man in Christ, we changed our place of residence. We see more and more of Beulah Land each time we go up— in the Spirit. But we still make pilgrimages to earth where He has appointed us to serve and reign as kings and priests, and where we have temporary housing. We decided not to remain as prodigals— outside the gates. We dwell in Zion now— the holy city of both our birth and rebirth. We are the chosen children of God, born to glorify our Lord Jesus on earth while we dwell with Him. It is not the other way around. We are kings and priests under His authority.

We are spiritually married to Him—therefore, one in Him. We are a special people— purified by our Savior's own blood. And because we are purified, we are holy. Yes, we are chosen— chosen to glorify God, to lift up the Name of Jesus wherever we are. To ensure that we focus our attention on what God desires for us to do every day before we attend to our precious early business, we need to go to Zion early each day before we become preoccupied. (Psalm 63:1). Each day we focus our attention on material things rather than on things of God is another day of the abundant life we lose.

We Are gods—
But We Must Declare Who We Are

> PSALM 82:6 "I say, "You are gods, sons of the Most High, all of you; but you shall die like men and fall as princes."

> JOHN 10:34 Accusing Him of blasphemy, Jesus answered them, "Is it not written in your law, 'I said, you are gods'?"

Whether we accept the truth or not is up to each one of us. We must choose to be gods. We must choose to be priests. We must choose to be kings— and we must be willing to reign as kings. Because Jesus came to earth in the flesh and declared His blessings upon us, we are the chosen generation of our Lord Jesus—the blessed generation. No, our genetic bloodline does not regard us as so, but our spiritline tells us the truth. Maybe this is the reason why everyday we hear the 'hum-drum' drill that we can't be holy because our genes carry the sins of Adam— and we can't have the higher gifts of healing and prophecy, speaking in tongues and the interpretation of tongues, and the discernment of spirits. "Don't you know that these gifts passed away with the end of the Apostolic Age?" they jeer. Pentecostal teachings allow for all of these gifts to function in the body of Christ. However, confusion reigns. Some say that a private prayer language is fine, but restrain utterances in church because there may not be an interpreter present; or, it's probably someone trying to edify himself, and it surely disrupts the flow of worship. There's nothing wrong with edifying ourselves, but our prayer language is personal. The gifts of prophecy, wisdom and knowledge are usually welcome in full gospel churches. It's best to know what regulations apply before we prophesy in church.

Yes, We Are 'Little Jesuses'

A dear pastor friend of ours took exception while we were all gathered together one evening in a prayer session when we declared, "We are Little Jesuses". And we are. I have also heard full gospel pastors say that there are no prophets living on earth today. Some pentecostal pastors have many of their flock still "tarrying at the altar". Worst of all, many Christians today have been taught and believe that Zion is unavailable to them until they take their last breath on earth. Lies, lies, and more lies. Such a mindset may as well say that God is a liar— that God's Word is in error— maybe the whole New Testament.

A defeated devil is having a heyday and living in apparent victory at the expense of Christians who will not accept the truth. Of course we are 'Little Jesuses'. Of course there are prophets on earth today. Jesus himself was a prophet; and the Father has given us all that He has, and made us joint heirs unto the Father (John 16:13-15;

Romans 8:17). This would surely include our ability to prophesy. Nothing has passed away.

We Inherited Our Spiritual Body When We Were Birthed

Examine the truth. When we were birthed in the Spirit, we inherited a spiritual body. Conversely, we also inherited a body of flesh that was contaminated by satan. God's perfect body of flesh became contaminated by Adam's sinful genetic composition from the moment we were birthed on earth. This birth in the flesh— with the genetic makeup of sinful Adam required us to be reborn in the Spirit lest our body of flesh in time would gain the upper hand, and rule over us indefinitely. Adam's fall from grace relegated mankind living under the Old Covenant to an unholy state of being— subject to the devil's authority on earth which he boldly proclaimed to Jesus during His forty days in the wilderness. But the devil's rule ended with Jesus' resurrection. Even before that happened, however, when Jesus went up after His Baptism in the Holy Spirit, He gained the strength to resist the devil's temptations. Matthew 4:1 records that Jesus was actually led into the wilderness by the Holy Spirit to be tempted. Surely satan knew he was in trouble when this occurred. Specifically, Luke 4:3-13, tells us that after Jesus had been baptized in the Holy Spirit and while in the wilderness, He was tempted three times by the devil— one of which was to offer Him the *"authority over all the kingdoms of the world and their glory; for it has been delivered to me, and I give it to whom I will. If you will worship me, it shall all be yours"* (Luke 4:6-7). But the devil could not break Jesus' will. Can he break ours? Not if we are in the Spirit.

The Devil Is Now Battling an Army of "Little Jesuses"

Throughout His ministry Jesus performed miracles that were not possible in man's mind. If satan had been able to keep mankind bottled up in his flesh, we would be losing every battle with him. However, when Jesus was resurrected, He sent the Holy Spirit to inhabit all believers. And this truth takes us back to Jesus' family history. In the Spirit, God reveals the difference in the genealogies in Matthew 1:1 & 1:2. With this insight comes the explanation for why God tells us in Psalm 82:6, "I say, you are gods." Gods? Yes, "Little Jesuses", when we have been empowered by the Holy Spirit to go into battle against evil. Our Father said so.

The genealogy of Jesus as recorded in Matthew 1:1, with mention only of David and Abraham, is repeated in reverse order beginning in Matthew 1:2. As listed in verses 2-16, we find in tracing Jesus' genealogy through the generations that this is actually the family tree of Joseph, Jesus' stepfather. This genealogy is supposedly a physical representation of "blood kin", just as we might find today in tracing our own "family tree". However, to establish a true physical "blood kin" genealogy for Jesus, we should study another source, Luke 3:23-38. A closer look tells us this is His mother Mary's lineage, still a physical genealogy, but an accurate one of our King and High Priest.

Noah's Righteousness Was Blameless

Closely examine how we are regarded in God's spiritual genealogy. While most believers today are not descendents of the bloodline of Noah's son Shem, which would make us Jews genetically, by bloodline (Genesis 10:21-31), we are all descendants of Noah spiritually. And, as Genesis 6:9 records, Noah was a righteous man, blameless in his generation; and Noah walked with God. Noah's flesh was not blameless, his righteousness was blameless. This insight gives us an even better understanding of our relationship and standing with God the Father as His "adopted children", entitled to the promise — not by bloodline, but by faith in His Word — and, therefore, we are God's sons and daughters of righteousness.

For we know from His Word, as recorded for us in Romans 8:14-17, "*All who are led by the Spirit of God are Sons of God. When we cry 'Abba Father.' it is the Holy Spirit bearing witness with our spirit that we are children of God, and if children, then heirs and fellow heirs with Christ provided we suffer with Him".*

Abraham's Righteousness Gives Us the Right to Bless Ourselves

ROMANS 4:11 Abraham is the father of all those who believe.

We know that God called Abraham in Genesis 12:1-3, telling him, *"I will make of you a great nation, and I will bless you and make your name great, so that you will be a blessing...and by you all the families of the earth shall bless themselves."* How can we bless ourselves unless we are ordained by God to do so? But we are so blessed. Examine how this is so. Obviously Abraham's physical bloodline is limited to the house of Israel, traced back to Noah and his son Shem. However, Abraham's spiritual fatherhood is the subject of the Apostle Paul's letter to the Romans in Romans 4:11, when he writes, *"Abraham is the "Father of those who believe, of both the circumcised and uncircumcised."* Jesus declares himself as Abraham's creator in John 8:58, saying, *"Truly, truly, I say to you, before Abraham was, I am"*, and also speaks of Abraham's rejoicing that he was able to see the day of the Lord and the New Covenant Generation (John 8:56). Today Christians recognize "Father Abraham" as an exemplary model of a spiritual father because of his obedience to God when he was willing to go to a faraway land and offer his son Isaac as a living sacrifice. This obedience was reckoned to

Abraham as righteousness, declared by Christ Jesus as our inheritance in Zion that we receive by faith (Genesis 12:1-3).

Our Blessings Have Been Declared by the Father, Son and Holy Spirit

GENESIS 12:1-3 Now the Lord said to Abram, "Go from your country and your kindred and your Father's house to the land that I will show you. And I will make of you a great nation, and I will bless you, and make your name great, so that you will be a blessing. I will bless those who bless you, and him who curses you I will curse; and by you all the families of the earth shall bless themselves."

JOHN 10:10 "The thief comes only to steal and kill and destroy; I came that they who believe in Me by their words may have life, and have it abundantly."

JOHN 16:13-15 "When the Spirit of Truth comes, He will guide you into all the truth; for He will not speak on His Own authority, but whatever He hears He will speak, and He will declare to you the things that are to come. He will glorify Me for He will take what is Mine and declare it to you. All that the Father has is Mine; therefore, I said that He will take what is Mine and declare it to you."

ROMANS 8:15-17 "When we cry, 'Abba, Father', It is the Spirit Himself bearing witness with our spirit that we are children of God, and if children, then heirs, heirs of God and fellow heirs with Christ Jesus, provided we suffer with Him in order that we may also be glorified with Him."

We should always be mindful of our inheritance as joint heirs with Jesus. We really have declarations by God the Father, Son, and Holy Spirit that our inheritance is in Zion waiting for our faith to claim and lay hold of it. It is just a matter of "connecting the dots". The Apostle Paul also declares it as so (Romans 8:17). At the Last Supper, our Lord Jesus promises His disciples that *"when the Holy Spirit comes He will glorify Me for He will take what is Mine and declare it to you"* (John 16:14). Jesus died on the cross at Calvary; but before He died, He made out a will; and, as this verse confirms, He declared what belonged to Him to be ours after His death. Yes, ours. This is our inheritance with all the saints in Zion— as joint heirs with Jesus, some of which represents the abundant life which He also declared as ours in this age (John 10:10). In John 17:20-24, we hear Jesus praying the Father for this dowry of blessings for His bride (SS 2:16; John 3:29) to be available not only to the eleven, but to the entire New Covenant Generation *"who believe in Me through their words"*— that we may all be one in Him and the Father and Them in us; and that we may be with Him where He is (John 17:20-24). His prayer was for us— His disciples in this age.

It is so important for us to remember that all these blessings are ours, by faith. This faith is the righteousness of our spirit man which we shield so carefully with the breastplate of righteousness when we put on the whole armor of God as we battle evil on earth (Eph. 6:14). When the Father declared to Abraham that all the families of the earth shall bless themselves, He was declaring blessings upon future generations of the New Covenant— not upon future generations of Old Covenant families who could not bless themselves in the spirit realm. Why not? Because our Lord Jesus had not come, lived and died, making us His heirs by His spoken and written will; and of course the Holy Spirit had not yet come into the hearts of men to declare it so. The Apostle Paul's declaration in Romans 8 that we are joint heirs— not "will be" joint heirs, means that we can enjoy some of our inheritance now, in this age; and infinitely magnanimous, eternal blessings in the Age of Jubilee. What an inheritance we have to enjoy in this life and the next.

Jesus Is the Cornerstone of Our Faith

Sometimes in this life we give in to our flesh, and the demands of the world's system test our faith. When this occurs, we should quickly remember that we are like Peter, living stones upon which Christ Jesus is building His church. As recorded for us in Matthew 16:15-18, when our Lord asked Simon Peter, *"Who do you say I am?"* And Peter answered, *"You are the Christ, the Son of the Living God."* Jesus answered him, *"You are Peter, and, on this rock I will build my church; and the gates of hell shall not prevail against it."* We are rocks on which Jesus is building His church. We know from reading I Peter 2:5-6 that the apostle has declared us to be living stones, built into the spiritual house of God— to be a holy priesthood, offering spiritual sacrifices to God the Father through Christ Jesus, our Lord and Savior. And those who believe in Him shall not be put to shame.

As recorded for us in Genesis 28:10-27, in a dream, our forefather Jacob dreamed of angels ascending and descending upon a ladder set on earth; and God spoke to him, repeating what He had declared to his grandfather Abraham two generations before him, that *"by you and your descendants, all the families of the earth shall bless themselves."* And when he awakened Jacob knew that the stone on which he had laid his head was a foundation stone of God's house and the gate to heaven.

We are that spiritual house. And we know that the stone on which Jacob laid his head represents the cornerstone of our faith— of our righteousness, Christ Jesus Himself. He is the stone which the builders rejected, a stone which has been laid in Zion, and we who believe in Him will not be put to shame (Psalm 118:22; Isaiah 28:16; Acts 4:11; Romans 9:33). He is clad in a robe dipped in blood, and the *"The Word of God" is the name by which He is called…On His robe and on His thigh He has a name inscribed, "King of kings and Lord of lords"* (Revelation 19:13-16). He is the cornerstone of our righteousness, the Head of the body of the church, and the pioneer of our faith;

He is our High Priest and as such all of our spiritual power and authority comes from Him. And, as recorded in I Peter 2:4-9, we have been called and chosen— if we accept the call, by Christ Jesus Himself, to be his kings and lords, *"Come to Him, to that living stone, rejected by men but in God's sight chosen and precious; and like living stones be yourselves built into a spiritual house, to be a holy priesthood, to offer spiritual sacrifices to God through Jesus Christ— the Cornerstone laid up in Zion...You are a chosen race, a royal priesthood, a holy nation, God's own people, that you may declare the wonderful deeds of Him who called you out of darkness into His marvelous light."* We are living stones to make up the body of the church; Jesus is the Head— the Cornerstone of our righteousness.

In Psalm 106:31, David prophesies about the genealogy of Jesus, saying that faith in God is reckoned as righteousness from generation to generation forever. Christ Jesus is the very Cornerstone of our existence. Never forget that He is our Creator, that He said in John 8:58, *"before Abraham, I am"*. And because of who we are, none of the curses that befell Adam can come upon us when we are in the spiritual realm in which Christ Jesus now resides.

My Soul Longs for the Peace of God— Found Only in Zion

Many years ago I found comfort in Lamentations 3:21-23, *But this I call to mind, and therefore I have hope: the steadfast love of the Lord never ceases; His mercies never end; they are new every morning, "Great is Thy faithfulness."* This passage always helped me to get over some problem that had bothered me the day before. Now, in the Spirit, I appreciate the passage so much more, and always add the next two verses to complete the full meaning and application to my circumstances: *"The Lord is my portion," says my soul, "therefore I will hope in Him." The Lord is good to those who wait for Him, to the soul who seeks Him* (Lamentations 3:24-25). I have found that if I take my soul to Zion with me each time I go to His throne room, God invites me to *"Come, let us reason together"* (Isaiah 1:18); and we converse together. Yes, that will be the way it is when we return to Zion permanently. We can have that sweet converse with God now.

Christians who have received the Baptism that John the Baptist could not give, are eager to receive and accept the commission Jesus gave them in Matthew 28:18-20, *"Go and make disciples of all nations, baptizing them in the Name of the Father, and of the Son, and of the Holy Spirit."* Our Lord Jesus has given us a charge— to disciple His sheep so they too can have what we have— the outpouring of the Holy Spirit, a semblance of the same outpouring Jesus himself received when He came up out of the water after being baptized by John the Baptist in the River Jordan. After His water baptism and while he was praying, the Holy Spirit descended upon Him in bodily form, as a dove, and a voice came to Him from heaven, saying, *"Thou art My Beloved Son; with Thee I am well pleased"* (Luke 3:21-22).

We Can Bless Ourselves

GENESIS 12:3 "I will bless those who bless you, and him who curses you I will curse; and by you all the families of the earth will bless themselves."

Yes, as difficult as it may be for us to comprehend, as "little Jesuses", we can pray for and bless ourselves. When God called Abraham, He told him, *"I will make of you a great nation... And by you all the families of the earth shall bless themselves"* (Genesis 12:2-3). What did God mean by this declaration? He was referring to Abraham's faith— reckoned to Him as righteousness. Our righteousness is like unto that of "Father Abraham". Our faith in Jesus as Lord establishes our right standing with God. This is why prayer works so effectively. We bless ourselves each and every time we use the Name of Jesus in prayer, sealing our decrees, and professing Him to the nations. Abraham believed God, period. And this obedience is one principle of prosperity that is always in effect for believers; and our lack of knowledge in applying this principle is of little comfort when we fail to please God. Conversely, our addiction to things of the flesh and the physical realm will only lead us to defeat and we will perish spiritually as prophesied by the prophet Hosea (Hosea 4:6). The Apostle Paul enumerates the works of the flesh in Galatians 5:20-21, *"idolatry, immorality, enmity, strife, jealousy, anger, drunkenness, carousing and the like;"* and reminds us that anyone who participates in such things cannot enter the Kingdom of Heaven. Idolatry seems to be the root cause of such habits and cravings because we put whatever has entrapped us ahead of God— trying to serve two masters as Jesus sternly warns us cannot be done (Matthew 6:24).

We Always Have a Choice

God reminds us in Malachi 3:10-12 of the abundant blessings of tithing and giving offerings, but also of the curse for robbing Him of what belongs to Him. Mark 4 plainly instructs us that the Word cannot produce in our lives if we are entrapped by our flesh— *"the cares of this world, the deceitfulness of riches, and the desire for other things"* (Mark 4:19). All such teachings are vitally important to us because we must be careful not to fall under the curse that Adam brought upon us all and lose our reward of the abundant life in this lifetime. We can do this with the fire of the anointing of the Holy Spirit. When we receive the Baptism in the Holy Spirit, we receive a good endowment from on high— His anointing; and we remain faithful to the giver of such a powerful gift.

Without this baptism, we cannot stand against our enemy. We have no battle armor. We cannot go to Zion because we don't know how to get there. We cannot receive our commission because we are not equipped to discharge it. Yes, we have received the precious gift of salvation out of God's deep love and compassion for us, but we are powerless to bless ourselves and earn our reward of the abundant life here on earth. And since we have not been baptized with fire, we are at best a one-talent man or woman (Matthew 25:15). God does not dare trust us with any more responsibility than that. We cannot call ourselves chosen because we have not yet gone back home to Zion to utilize the endowed power and authority from on high we need to prosper on earth. We know from the Book of Jeremiah that God revealed his predetermined will for the prophet, saying, *"Before I formed you in the womb I knew you, and before you were born I consecrated you; and appointed you a prophet to the nations"* (Jeremiah 1:5). Isaiah 55:11 tells us God has declared, *"My Word that goes forth from My mouth shall not return to Me void, but it shall accomplish that which I purpose, and prosper in the thing for which I sent it."*

The Anointing Enables
Us to "Go Up" to Zion

JAMES 1:17 Every good endowment and every perfect gift is from above, coming down from the Father of Lights, with Whom there is no variation or shadow due to change.

When Christ Jesus baptizes God's people in the Holy Spirit, without any variation as to who we are in Jerusalem, the anointed endowment of power and authority we receive from on high is a lesser amount of the same perfect endowment Jesus received after He came up from the water in the River Jordan. Luke 3:21-22 records it this way: *When all the people were baptized, and when Jesus also had been baptized, heaven was opened and the Holy Spirit descended upon Him in bodily form, as a dove, and a voice came from heaven, "Thou art My Beloved Son; with Thee I am well pleased."* Matthew 3:16 and 4:1 tells us, *And when Jesus was baptized, He went up immediately from the water, and behold, the heavens were opened and He saw the Spirit of God descending like a dove, and alighting on Him; and lo, a voice from heaven,* saying, *"This is My Beloved Son, with Whom I am well pleased".* Then Jesus was led up by the Holy Spirit into the wilderness to be tempted by the devil. Twice in these three verses, the Word records that Jesus went up.

Acts 10:34-43 records Peter's sermon about the life of Jesus to Cornelius, a Roman centurion who would thereafter receive the Baptism in the Holy Spirit together with other gentiles. Concerning the occasion of Jesus' Baptism in the Holy Spirit after His water baptism by John the Baptist in the River Jordan, Peter said to Cornelius and the others in verse 38, *"God anointed Jesus of Nazareth with the Holy Spirit and with power; and He went about doing good and healing all that were oppressed by the devil, for God was with Him."*

The importance of these events cannot be overemphasized. Without the power of the anointing given by God to Jesus at the River Jordan and to all of us who also receive the Baptism in the Holy Spirit we cannot stand against the devil. Ask yourself this question: "Would Jesus have been led by the Holy Spirit into the wilderness to be tempted by the devil if He had not received the anointing"? We know that Jesus prayed the Father at the Last Supper that we have everything that He has (John 16:15). Therefore, knowing that this baptism is not available on earth — that it is a gift of God from Zion — and we can receive it only if we are in the Spirit, we know Jesus wants us to *Mount Up to Zion.* He laid down His life for us at Calvary; therefore we know Jesus yearns for His anointing to be given to us, His friends who do what He commands us to do (John 15:13-14).

The Davidic Covenant —
Our Kingship and Royal Priesthood

I SAMUEL 16:1 "I have rejected Saul from being king over Israel. Fill your horn with oil and go to Jesse the Bethlehemite, for I have provided for Myself a king among his sons.**

I Samuel 16 tells the familiar story of how God anointed David as king of Israel long before he was crowned — He declared it so. Jesse paraded seven of his sons before Samuel — except of course for David, his youngest and a mere shepherd boy. And yet he had to send for David before Samuel could anoint God's chosen one as king. There is no way David had a legal right to Saul's throne — it would have been appropriate for Saul's eldest son to assume the throne upon Saul's death. Remember: at this time Saul was still sitting on the throne; and his eldest son, Jonathan, and his two brothers, were very much alive. But God knew that Saul and all three of his sons would be slain in battle, as recorded in I Samuel 31:1-8, and Saul would therefore leave no heir. And we know that when David slew Goliath his popularity soared with the people. I Samuel 18:7 tells us, the women began chanting, *"Saul has slain his thousands, and David his ten thousands."* So, as expected, after Saul's death — as well as the deaths of Jonathan and his brothers, David came home triumphantly after defeating the

Amalekites, received the anointing of men and was declared king by the people.

However, David's anointing by Samuel well before Saul died tells us that God himself decides who is royalty— who is to serve Him on earth as a king. Yes, the circumstances aligned themselves, but when God declared and anointed David the shepherd boy as king, the question was not whether David would be king, but rather when it would occur— on His timetable. So it is with each of us. When we are baptized in the Holy Spirit we receive God's anointing— just as David received it. And we receive a portion of what Jesus the Anointed One received when He came up out of the River Jordan after being baptized by John the Baptist. We ask ourselves: "Why did God choose us to receive the anointing?" But we already know the answer: we have made our Father proud of us. Behold— He is well pleased.

We Can't Lose God's Gift of salvation— But We Can Lose the Anointing

Just as it is hard to think of King David as a vassal king of God the Father, the Supreme King, he was just that— just as we are vassals of King Jesus on earth— provided we continue to abide in Him. While we cannot lose our salvation, we can lose our anointing. King Saul lost the anointing. No, he did not lose his salvation. He was still God's child, but he was no longer able to exercise spiritual power— no longer was he King of Israel in God's eyes— remember that Samuel had anointed David as the new king of Israel.

And we know what happened to Saul when we read the account in I Samuel 16:14, *Now the Spirit of the Lord departed from Saul, and an evil spirit from the Lord tormented him.* And, although we know that Saul was still physically sitting on the throne, after David slew Goliath, Saul relentlessly pursued David to kill him. And, as his final demise drew near, and Saul realized the Philistines were coming to war against Israel, he became very afraid and asked God to help him. But when he inquired of the Lord, the Lord did not answer him, either by dreams or by Urim, or by the prophets— forcing him to seek advice from a medium. The result was fatal for him and his sons— and Saul's body was decapitated by the Philistines (I Samuel 31:2, 8-9).

King Solomon's situation was very similar, and yet much worse in many ways. We read in I Kings 11, that when Solomon turned away from God, taking foreign wives who turned his heart away from God and even went after abominable things, God told him, *"Since this has been your mind and you have not kept My covenant and My commandments, I will surely tear the kingdom away from you and give it to your servant. However, for the sake of your father David, I will not do this during your days; but I will take it away from your son; except for one tribe (Judah) for the sake of David and Jerusalem which I have chosen"*. And the Lord raised up adversaries against Solomon— including Jeroboam, the son of Nebat, a servant of Solomon who would become king of the northern kingdom of Israel (I Kings 11:1-40). And although we are not told that Solomon lost his anointing completely, the fact that Solomon took foreign wives (700 wives and princesses, and 300 concubines) who turned his heart away from God to foreign gods, and he did what was evil in God's eyes, God raised up adversaries against him— and hardened Solomon's heart against Jereboam, whom God himself had raised up to become king of Israel, tells us that Solomon's anointing was greatly diminished.

Solomon was inspired to write the Book of Ecclesiastes late in his life— primarily as a lesson, warning man of what we lose when we turn away from God. We know that Solomon himself knew the pain, vanity, and emptiness of a life of sorrow and guilt. He was once blessed with great wisdom and wealth— only to lose it to a carnal lifestyle: *"For to the man who pleases him God gives wisdom and knowledge and joy; but to the sinner God gives work of gathering and heaping, only to give to one who pleases Him"* (Ecclesiastes 2:26).

Ecclesiastes 1:9-17 describes Solomon's demeanor in his latter years as a broken man who once had it all. As he reflected back on all of his greatness, it seemed as vanity to a man whose life had not only lost meaning but who now hated life *"because what is done under the sun was grievous to me"*. A spiritually broken man, Solomon had lost his relationship with God— and with it, the meaning of life. Our obedience to God means our anointing is for today and forever.

It was not like God had not warned Solomon about the consequences. Before he died and Solomon became king, his father David warned Solomon that disobedience to God would cost his lineage the throne— although God had established Solomon's kingdom forever (II Samuel 7:13). Solomon and his lineage would be answerable to God; and just as God had told David, Solomon's lineage's right of entitlement to the throne of Israel was conditional. David warned Solomon about what God had told him, *"If your sons keep My covenant and My testimonies, and take heed to their way, walking before Me in faithfulness with all their heart and with all their soul, there shall not fail you a man on the throne of Israel"* (Psalm 132:12; First Kings 2:4). But Solomon's sins found him out when his heart turned away from God, and David's warning became prophecy. After Solomon turned away from God, God told Solomon that the kingdom would be taken away from his lineage and given to his servant, except for the House of Judah because of his father (I Kings 11:9-13). We know this is exactly what happened. The division of the kingdom occurred under Solomon's son Rehoboam's rule. And just as God had warned David and so advised Solomon, God allowed the throne of the northern kingdom of Israel to be given over to Jeroboam, the son of Nebat, a servant of Solomon. This kingdom ceased to exist under the Assyrian siege and Israel's exile (II Kings 17:21-24).

What Happened to the Throne of David?

However, God allowed the kingdom of Judah— the throne of David, to continue until the rule of King Jeconiah. Jeconiah's evil ways provoked Him so much that God removed the signet ring from his finger and took the kingdom away from him (Jeremiah 22:24-30). Thus, the Curse of Jeconiah, which was really due to the sins of Solomon, came upon evil King Zedekiah of Judah after Jeconiah, who ruled but 90 days, was taken into exile by Nebuchadnezzar, the Babylonian king. Zedekiah, appointed by Nebuchdnezzar himself to rule in Jerusalem, became the last king of Judah— officially, when after ruling for eleven years (II Kings:24:18), the Babylonians slew all Zedekiah's sons before his eyes and gouged out his eyes— binding him in fetters and taking him captive (Jeremiah 39:6-7).

We will examine how God removed this curse when we again focus on the Kingship and Lordship of Christ Jesus in our discussion of sealing a decision we make on earth with the Signet Ring. At this time, for the purpose of discussing our own kingship under the Davidic Covenant, it is important that we remember God removed this curse when He chose Jeconiah's grandson, Zerubbabel— the governor of Judah and part of the 40,000 remnant, to "wear the signet ring". As recorded in Haggai 2:21-23, we hear God speaking to the prophet, *"Speak to Zerubbabel, governor of Judah, saying, I am about to shake the heavens and the earth, and to overthrow the throne of kingdoms...on that day, I will take you, O Zerubbabel, My servant, and make you like a signet ring, for I have chosen you," says the Lord of hosts.*

Zerubbabel's Restoration Proves That God Anoints Whom He Wills

How can this be?' we first ask ourselves. "Is God saying here that no longer is the curse of the fathers visited upon the sons?" Yes. The Book of Haggai is a call by God for the Jewish people to rebuild the Temple of Solomon. They had been in captivity for seventy years but began returning to their homeland to rebuild Jerusalem by the edict of King Cyrus of Persia in 535 B.C. when 40,000 were allowed to go home to Jerusalem under the leadership of Zerubbabel, recognized not as a king in a physical sense, but rather as the governor of a people in captivity, and by Jeshua the High Priest. Later King Darius freed the remainder of the captive Jewish people (521 B.C.).

Zerubbabel's Restoration Proves That Jesus Is King and Lord

Zerubbabel's restoration to the Throne of Israel and to kingly power is like unto God anointing David as King of Israel while Saul still sat on the throne (First Samuel 16:13-14). Except in Zerubbabel's case, there was no sitting king of Israel or Judah. But by examining Zerubbabel's lineage closely it gives us the proof we need to show that Jesus is King and Lord— that God anoints whom He wills and chooses to be both a king and lord. As we review Zerubbabel's restoration, we closely examine references in the Book of Hebrews to support our study of Jesus as our King and our High Priest.

Our Royal Priesthood

HEBREWS 2:7-8 God has crowned Jesus with glory and honor, putting everything in subjection under His feet.

We have been studying Matthew 1:1 as a confirmation of the spiritual genealogy of Jesus Christ, or the chosen New Covenant Generation of Jesus Christ. Why is this so important? Because using physical facts, we cannot dismiss or explain away the curse that befalls all descendants of Adam. His genetics have contaminated the genes of mankind. We must keep in mind as we examine the difference in these genealogies that Hebrews 5 records a change in the priesthood together with a change in the covenant. We can trace Jesus' mother Mary's lineage back to David realizing that Jesus is now our High Priest of the New Covenant, appointed not by man, but by God Himself who declared that Jesus would hold the office permanently. God swears it and inspired David to write it in Psalm 110:4, saying, *"I have sworn, and I will not change My mind, you who sits at My right hand are a priest forever, after the order of Melchizedek."* What does this mean for us? With Jesus now seated at our Father's right hand, we can be seated at our Lord Jesus' right hand. He is our Chief Priest— and we are His priests.

God Changed His Mind About the Priesthood— Yes, We Are Priests

God's sworn declaration as recorded in Psalm 110:4 does not comply with His perpetual statute establishing the Levitical priesthood to be held by Aaron and his sons, and his descendants after him that God declared to Moses in Exodus 28:43 & 29:9. We know that Abraham paid tithes to Melchizedek, king of Salem, and he received Melchizedek's blessing (Genesis 14:18-20), and that Jesus' ordination as our High Priest is not after the Levitical order, but rather Melchizedek's order. Although Melchizedek's lineage cannot be traced, God obviously changed His mind about the priesthood. His Old Covenant legal requirement that priests be appointed by man from the Levitical order was changed when Jesus came to earth. John the Baptist, often referred to as the last Levitical priest, was well aware of the priestly authority of Jesus. In Luke 3:16, John the Baptist proclaims this authority to the people, *"I baptize you with water; but He Who is mightier than I is coming, the thong of whose sandals I am not worthy to untie; He will baptize you with the Holy Spirit and with fire."* And in Matthew 3:13-14, when Jesus came to be baptized in the River Jordan by John the Baptist, scripture records, John would have prevented Him, saying, *"I need to be baptized by You, and do You come to me?"* But Jesus answered him, saying, *"Let it be so now; for thus it is fitting for us to fulfill all righteousness."*

Jesus is our High Priest forever. In addition to our study of Melchazedek, we also need to reference the Lordship of Jeshua — the son of Jehozadak, the High Priest. Zechariah 6:11-14 records how Joshua (Jeshua, Yeshua, Jesus) was crowned by Zechariah as a type of the Branch, and, as prophesied by the prophet, the Branch shall grow up in his place and build a temple to the Lord, shall bear royal honor, and shall sit and rule upon His throne. God determined that whosoever believes in Him as Lord and Savior is both born of His Spirit and washed in His blood; and, while we are not His "physical blood kin" in a legal sense because Jesus fathered no children in the natural, we are His children — and His brethren — His "spiritual blood kin" by covenant. We realize that King David performed priestly duties, blessing the people in the Name of the Lord. He appointed Levites as ministers to God, and led the festal shout when the Ark of the Covenant was returned to Jerusalem and placed inside the tent he had pitched. And the king received offerings and distributed food to the people (I Chronicles 16:1-6).

David's Anointing by Samuel
Was Spiritual — Just as Ours

It is of great significance that David is a key figure in Jesus' spiritual genealogy. Selected by God from all of Jesse's sons, as prophesied by the prophet Isaiah (Isaiah 11:1), the prophet Samuel anointed David, the stump of Jesse, as king of Israel long before he was actually crowned by man. God reminded Samuel that man looked on things of the flesh, but He regarded the inner man. David's anointing was spiritual — and the Spirit of the Lord came mightily upon David from that day forward (I Samuel 16:7-13). David wrote Psalm 110, prophesying the coming of Jesus as the Messiah and establishing Jesus as High Priest after the order of Melchizedek. Based upon this prophecy, we know that David declared himself to be a priest as well as king of Israel as recorded in I Chronicles 15:27 and 16:6, when he, together with the elders of Israel and his commanders of thousands, brought the ark of the covenant of the

Lord back to Jerusalem since it had been removed because of neglect during Saul's reign; and David clothed himself like all the Levites, wearing a fine linen robe and wearing an ephod symbolic of priestly authority; danced before the Lord; offered offerings; blessed and fed the people; and had the ark placed in the tent tabernacle he himself had pitched for it. And King David himself prophesied in I Chronicles 16:13, calling the people *"offspring of Abraham and sons of Jacob, God's chosen ones."* This prophecy makes us the chosen ones— the chosen generation of the New Covenant in Christ Jesus.

David Was a Forerunner of the Messiah— Our Oneness in Christ

This message from God established the Davidic Covenant whereby David knew himself to be the forerunner of the promise. Of course, this prophecy is the inheritance of the saints— our imperishable gift of oneness in Christ— the Son of David, and recognizes us as both kings and priests, as declared by covenant. If our genealogy is physical, it is of the flesh; and therefore cursed— genetic and laden with sin, disease, unbelief, and bondage. Yes, we can prove that we are the spiritual children of Noah— and of Abraham, by adoption. But since our genealogy is spiritual, of the Holy Spirit, with Jesus as the cornerstone, and therefore blessed, we can bless ourselves (Genesis 12:3).

We bless ourselves by putting our faith to work. James 2:17-26 teaches us, *Faith by itself without works is dead.* Since we are children of Abraham by faith, we know that he was justified by works of faith when he offered his son, Isaac, upon the altar. God expects us to be willing to act in faith— even if what He asks of us doesn't seem the right thing to do. Abraham believed that somehow God would spare Isaac because he was the child of the promise; but Abraham obeyed God and Isaac was spared.

"Not by Power Nor by Might, But by My Spirit"

PSALM 84:5-9 **"Blessed are the men whose strength is in Thee, and in whose heart is the highway to Zion...They go from strength to strength; the God of gods will be seen in Zion. O Lord God of hosts, hear my prayer and look upon the face of thy anointed."**

When we are endowed with the good gift of salvation from above that Jesus made possible by His Own blood, given to us by the Father of Lights (James 1:17), and the Holy Spirit enters into us, only then are we prepared to receive His Baptism and the power of the anointing necessary to accept and discharge our God-given commission. And how and where are we to receive this perfect gift of the anointing if not by faith from above? We cannot. We must be in Zion. God does not faint or grow weary by striving to accomplish His purpose by physical power or might. No, His purpose is manifested on earth *"by My Spirit,"* saith the Lord. (Zechariah 4:6). Nor will God allow us to use our own power and might to have the things we hope for by striving after them— even if sometimes we feel we can. Yes, God does strengthen our might but He also knows our physical limitations. God's instructions are clear: He wants us to wait for Him— for His Holy Spirit to bring us to Zion and receive strength from on high— and, as we draw near to Him we begin to renew our own strength, steadily mounting up with wings as eagles (Isaiah 40:31), and He draws closer to us until we are one in the Spirit. And we declare it so from our own mouths.

Jesus Has Prepared a Place for Us in Zion

JOHN 10:9 "I am the Door; if anyone comes in by Me, he will be saved, and will go in and out and find pasture."

When Jesus ascended into heaven, He prepared a place for us there, in our homeland (John 14:3 & 17:24)— not just for when we take our last breath here on earth, but to converse with Him daily and grant us access to God the Father. As the new creation we are— a new man in Christ (II Corinthians 5:17), God wants us to ditch our old habits and get in the new habit of going home in this life— this means that we "go up" in the Spirit. Jesus resides in Zion where He sits at the Father's right hand. He is our High Priest of the New Covenant who makes constant intercession for us, offering His Own blood— the perfect sacrifice for the remission of our sins and for our constant purification (Romans 8:34; Hebrews 5:1-10). He has us as His bride— we are His friends and we rejoice at the sound of His voice. He promises us the eternal commitment of a faithful Bridegroom, and an enduring friendship only a best friend can offer (John 3:29).

Maybe you have asked yourself, "Why do I need to go to Zion today? I'll just wait until it's my time to go". More likely you've said, "What I wouldn't give just to be in Zion for just one day." Read John 10 & John 17 carefully. Listen with your spiritual ears. Don't you recognize His voice? Listen closely. He is calling your name. Does it make any sense that our best Friend would be calling our name if we have already been found and He'll just have to wait and see us in the sweet bye and bye? Do you think? While we wander about in the pasture or are lured away, do you think He is going to just let us go our own way? No, never. We are God's children and joint heirs with Him of the Kingdom of God. Jesus wants us close to Him everyday so that He can reveal the secrets of the Kingdom to us. He wants us to remain in His pasture— in Zion and in our own little Jerusalem where we have temporarily pitched a tent and camped out.

Jesus Calls Us to Be His Bride

Our Husband wants us to be where He is, and we hear and recognize His voice calling our name.. John 10 is much about Jesus as the Good Shepherd and us as His sheep— who hear His voice calling our name, and we follow Him. Jesus declares in John 10:14, *"I am the Good Shepherd; I know My Own and they know Me."* This is not merely a prayer for the eleven to be with Him in Zion. Reason would tell us that. But in John 17:20, Jesus makes it clear that He is praying for all New Covenant believers when He declares, *"I do not pray for these only, but also for those who believe in Me by their word."* So, surely we can find any number of reasons why we may need to *Have a Little Talk with Jesus* to tell Him about our troubles, or about anything we may want to discuss with our best Friend— including sharing any need with Him. Or perhaps we need to present ourselves to the Father for much needed "fatherly advice"— to seek forgiveness for a sinful situation in our life that threatens our relationship with Him, to adjust our battle armor to help us stand against our enemy, to request healing for a friend or family member, to pray for a person to receive the gift of salvation, to discuss particulars about our commission or an appointed task God has asked us to do, to get an answer to a nagging family problem or situation, to find a solution to a money problem, to help us make a decision about a job or career move we are contemplating, to help us get through grief and depression during a trying time in our life, to stand in the gap for a friend or family member, to help us to forgive a friend or neighbor who has done us wrong, to repair a broken relationship with a family member, to thank Him for all that He has done for us or for a specific thing that we feel the need to give testimony, or just to tell Him how much we love Him.

We Are God's Children
But Too Often Try to "Pull Our Own Strings"

No matter how old we are, the cravings of our flesh often hinder our understanding of the importance of "going home". Despite our constant need for divine inspiration and for God's direct intervention when we go astray to lead us in the Way and the Truth so that we might enjoy God's best, His perfect will operating in our lives, we must go home to Zion to have our strength renewed and receive our Father's counsel. Whether we admit it or not, we need our Father's counsel in the Spirit to help us with our big decisions. Too often we think we can "pull our own strings" and miss out on God's perfect will — and what a miss it is.

Receiving the Baptism in the Holy Spirit

The only way we know for certain that we have received the Baptism is to experience the gifts of the Spirit and the full operation of the Gospel of

Jesus Christ working in our lives, with the evidence of speaking in tongues. Only then do we know with certainty that the prophet Joel's prophecy will have come to pass in our lives, that God has poured out His Spirit on our flesh, so that we can prophesy, dream dreams and see visions (Joel 2:28). And then we know that Psalm 91 will have come to pass in our lives— that we are dwelling in the shelter of the Most High, abiding in the shadow of the Almighty (Psalm 91:1). And we know that what Paul wrote to Timothy as the Word of Truth has been manifested in him and us (II Timothy 4:18).

God the Father's gift of salvation saves us for eternal rest in His heavenly Kingdom, yes— a thousand times, yes. But He wants us to have the rewards of the abundant life on earth now— that Jesus came on earth to give us. And this life is available to us only in Zion. We also know with absolute certainty that the constancy of our daily presence in Zion now in this life is essential. The Baptism in the Holy Spirit enables us to exercise our rights as citizens of Zion and keeps us in God's perfect will.

One Day in Zion Is Better than a Thousand Elsewhere

PSALM 84:10 "A day in Thy courts is better than a thousand elsewhere."

Since we are children of God, our spirits yearn to be home. We know that despite the familiarity of everyday things that surround us in the natural realm, our homeland is Mount Zion. We serve a jealous God who does not care to wait until our time on earth is done before He sees us again. He wants and expects us to come to Zion for counsel. Despite our temporary dwelling place on earth, our true homeland is the Holy City of Zion on our Father's Holy Mount Zion. Our generation has the benefit of someone the men of old did not have— Christ Jesus. Because He came to earth in the flesh and defeated satan, we are the chosen generation.

Jesus offers His friendship to all whosoevers, no matter what our position may be on the world's social ladder and regardless of our economic status. We are all created equal in His and the Father's image, both of Whom are Spirit (Genesis 1:26), so we know that we are spirits. We profess, *"Jesus Is Lord"*, because He died for us and paid the ransom for our release from bondage (Mark 10:45); and He wants us with Him where He is (John 17:24). He made a way at Calvary for us to enjoy direct access to our equal opportunity Dad., created in His perfection, a polluted world made us imperfect and in need of His cleansing blood to rid ourselves of our unrighteousness— giving us a way to Zion. By His blood we were redeemed and our salvation was secured (John 3:16; Ephesians 1:7). The Apostle Paul confirms this truth in Colossians 1:13-14, *"we have been transferred from the dominion of darkness to the Kingdom of light."* And we know that if we walk in the light, as He is in the Light, and confess our sins before Jesus and the Father— in Zion, we will have fellowship with one another. We know that *"God is faithful and just, and will forgive our sins and cleanse us from all unrighteousness by the blood of Jesus His Son"* (I John 1:7-9).

We Are Cleansed and Highly Favored

This cleansing means that we have a heavenly home in Zion where God the Father awaits our arrival as His children. In Romans 8:15-16, the Apostle Paul writes, *"When we cry 'Abba, Father.' it is the Holy Spirit Himself bearing witness with our spirit that we are children of God and joint heirs with Christ, provided we suffer with Him in order to be glorified with Him."* I Peter 2:9 assures us that *"we are a blessed generation, and we have been called out of darkness into his marvelous light."* John 10 confirms Jesus as the Good Shepherd and the Door to Zion. Jesus declares to us in John 10:9, *"I am the Door; if anyone enters by Me, he will be saved, and will go in and out and find pasture."*

Within the text of the passages referenced above, we know that we have been greatly favored by God. How do we know? Because Jesus emphasizes what the Door means for us. First, we have been called out of the darkness that held our old man captive— just as it did the entire Old Covenant Generation, offering our new man in Christ the priceless gift of salvation. Because we know His voice and will follow no other (John 10:27), while we are yet sojourning on the earth Jesus assures our new man that He gives us eternal life and access to the Father in Zion by Him— the Door, now.

Blessed Assurance, Jesus Is Ours

Blessed Assurance, Jesus Is Mine is a favorite hymn of the ages. It is certainly one of mine. Jesus said that He would never leave us desolate— and He is a Man of His Word. He sent the Holy Spirit to our beloved and blessed generation— this is our story and this is our song. Because He lives in each of us, we live in Him and belong to Him. We have many assurances that He is ours because we know Him as Lord, Savior, Master. Acts 2:14-36 records Peter's Pentecostal Sermon to the men of Judea; and from verse 36, God's Word tells us, *Jesus is Lord.* We hear the apostle proclaiming, *"Let all the house of Israel know assuredly that God has made Him both Lord and Christ, this Jesus Whom you crucified."*

We know that Jesus resides in Zion now from his own affirmation during his trial before Pilate, *"My Kingdom is not of this world"* (John 18:36). We know that upon recognition of our sinful state and our confession that Jesus Is Lord, we have been born again of the Spirit of Christ (John 3:6). Therefore, we are not of this world — and we can reside now where He resides if we desire to do so and can operate in the realm of the Spirit if we are empowered to do so. In the words of the psalmist, *"He who dwells in the shelter of the Most High, who abides in the shadow of the Almighty, will say to the Lord, 'My Refuge and my Fortress; my God in Whom I trust'"* (Psalm 91:1).

God Desires Oneship with Us

EXODUS 34:14 "You shall serve no other god, for the Lord, whose name is Jealous, is a jealous God."

Throughout the Bible there is a strong emphasis on oneship in the Lord. This is why the courtship and beautiful love story in the Song of Solomon between the bride and her lover, the *Parable of the Marriage Feast* in Luke 14 and the *Parable of the Prodigal Son* in Luke 15, take on such importance to us. The tie that binds two spirits created in God's image and likeness is ours. As spirit beings, when we look at what our relationship with Him should be, it is easy to see what God intended when we were created. He has declared and purposed oneship in Him — that we all should be equally yoked — and forever bound together through mutual love and affection, faithfulness, trustworthiness and fidelity. Since the fall of Adam, God has determined that His family will come back together. This was the purpose of His search for Old Covenant shepherds, and, when they failed Him, He sent His Son Jesus to earth so that in and through Him, all mankind could be reconciled with their Creator. The only place this oneship can occur is in Zion where we were all birthed.

Follow the Ancient Paths

JEREMIAH 6:16 "Stand by in the ways, and see and ask for the ancient paths where the good way is, and walk in it, and you will find rest for your souls."

Noah, Abraham, Sarah, Isaac, Jacob, Moses, Joshua, David, the prophets, and all our other heroes of the Old Testament were created in the image and likeness of God just as we were created. Yes, God enjoyed a oneship with them on earth, although they were unable to go up to Zion. Jeremiah 6:16 is prophecy for us. We should always try to emulate their faith— follow them as they walked the ancient paths. As adopted sons and daughters of Abraham, we are entitled to be called God's Own people and we always remember our heritage.

Just like us, Old Covenant people were sinful, but they were condemned by the Law. But they had no redeemer— at least not until Jesus was crucified, forgave them, and freed them from hell's fire upon His resurrection. They had no way to have their bodies and souls forever cleansed from sin and unrighteousness by the blood of the Perfect Lamb of God. Thus oneship between God and the "most cleansed" and best beloved of these heroes was never possible. The blood of animals used for cleansing them was imperfect. If our forefathers had only known Jesus as Lord as we know Him today, many of them would have surely found the highway during their lifetime and would have traveled on to Zion for refuge daily.

Still, God tried to show them favor. He searched for and found good shepherds among the Old Covenant Generation — men and women He could trust, enter into covenant with, and upon whom He could shine the glorious light of his countenance so that His Word could accomplish that which He had declared it to do. God searched far and wide to find and anoint men and women of great faith whose hearts were blameless toward Him (II Chronicles16:9). In every case, Old Covenant man proved incapable of keeping the Law, and not only disappointed God, but ultimately lacked the abiding faith which kept them from enjoying the benefits of His favor.

Walk in the Spirit

GALATIANS 5:16-17 "This I say to you, walk in the Spirit and you shall not fulfill the lust of the flesh."

We must remember that we are a new creation in Christ, and the Father wants us to be in victory always. And to experience such victory, we must go to Zion— and we must be in the spirit realm to go to Zion. Being in our flesh and using only our physical senses is the same as reverting to our old man. Because just like the Old Covenant Generation, we can't get to Zion in the natural, physical realm— nor can we somehow take our flesh with us as an unstable double-minded man would, and expect anything from the Lord (James 1:7-8).

We must never forget the rules for worshiping the Father in Zion, as set forth in Psalm 100: *"Make a joyful noise unto the Lord, serve Him with gladness, come into His presence with singing for He made us and not we ourselves— and we are the sheep of His pasture; enter His gates with thanksgiving and His courts with praise."* We will never lose our way— on his Holy Mount Zion or inside the City. The Holy Spirit will carry us to the highway where Jesus will meet and take us through every door as we tour the City.

We Don't Want To Perish for Lack of Knowledge

Some of you who are reading this book might say, "I pray in church and in my prayer closet at home and I know God hears me. Is this the same as being in Zion?" No. You will know when you are in the Spirit. In such times, God will take over and

fill your being.   During the entire time I was a
salvation Christian— I was "good and saved", yes—
but was I ready for battle?   Hardly.   The trumpet
sound was always indistinct (I Corinthians 14:8) if I
heard it at all in all the years before I received the
Baptism of the Holy Spirit.   When my father died in
1966, it hit me hard, and I remember babbling about
something several times in my "talks with Jesus"—
unintelligible gibberish I thought at the time, but I
know now the Holy Spirit was trying His best to
speak to me in the Spirit if only I could have been
tuned in.   But at the time I was striving hard on an
insurance debit to "make ends meet", had many
other things on my mind, and my knowledge base
was severely limited.

Can We Envision the Bodies of the Saints Coming Out of Their Graves?

Members of the early church experienced terrible
opposition and unthinkable persecution from the
Pharisees (Jewish religious hierarchy) and the
Saducees (unbelievers). Still they could not wait to
tell somebody.   And they did— often in fear for
their very lives.   As Acts 4:31-32 tells us, when the
anointing of the Holy Spirit fell upon them, they
spoke the Word of God boldly, and were of one
heart and soul.   If you can envision this scene at
Calvary— the curtain in the Temple that separated
the people of the Old Covenant from the presence
of God being torn in two when Jesus yielded up
His Spirit; and many bodies of the saints who had

fallen asleep being raised, coming out of their tombs after His resurrection and going into Jerusalem where they appeared to many (Matthew 27:51-53), then surely you can envision yourself talking with the Master in Zion today. And as the words of that old familiar hymn ring in your ears, can you also visualize yourself actually having a *Little Talk with Jesus* while you are there? If so, you can certainly "go up". You will know then that you are on the highway to Zion. And walking in His garden. And hearing the joyful sound of the Festal Shout (Psalm 89:15). And walking hand-in-hand with Jesus in His Light on His Holy Mountain (Psalm 56:13). And feeling the presence of angels on the streets of the City? And standing in the courtyard beside our loved ones? And seeing and worshiping in the Temple the prophet Ezekiel describes for us when God set him down on Mount Zion on which he saw the Holy City opposite him. Remember? With Jesus as his guide, Ezekiel opened his spiritual eyes and ears, described the courts of the Temple; and actually walked through it, declaring everything he saw and heard to us. Can you envision feasting with the Festal Gathering (Hebrews 12:22-23) with Jesus beside you in the presence of the Father? Or actually feeling the hand of Jesus holding yours with His arms around you and embracing you— with His words of assurance that He will never leave you. Surely you will see and perhaps talk with some of the saints while you are there in the Spirit?

God's Favor — the Gift of a Shepherd

ROMANS 6:23 The wages of sin is death, but the gift of God is eternal life in Christ Jesus.

It is very important we remember that during the Creation, God's Spirit was moving over the face of the waters of an earth that was covered in darkness, without form and void of light (Genesis 1:2). So, God created light, saw that it was good, and separated it from the darkness (Genesis 1:3). We know that the light He created was and is Christ Jesus, His Beloved Son — created in His Own image and likeness, the first-born of all creation (Col. 1:15). From that moment until this, God has stood on his Word that it will not return to Him void, but that it will accomplish that which he purposed and declared it to do (Isaiah 55:11). In the beginning, to ensure that man would live in the perfection deserving of the perfect creation God made — in the very image and likeness of God the Father and God the Son, God established the Garden of Eden as a protected fortress of plenty where God and man could have daily fellowship. In addition to the trees and plants that provided Adam and Eve with daily sustenance for their physical bodies, both the tree of life and the forbidden tree of the knowledge of good and evil were in the garden. But when Adam and Eve failed Him, surrendering their God-given dominion on earth to the creeping things (Genesis 1:26) inhabited by darkness — the spiritual forces of wickedness in heavenly places (Ephesians 6:12), the entire Old Covenant

Generation was condemned to also fail Him. God separated himself from them; and, as a case in point, Moses was required to wear a veil in God's presence to show that no sinful man could ever look upon His face (Exodus 34:33). The burden of sin for generations upon generations, the entire age of that one generation as a whole was too heavy— and God could find no shepherd worthy of leading them back to their homeland where they could enjoy His everlasting presence. So, God would only visit with them for a time, but they could never come home. They were both physically and spiritually exiled from the freedom of their homeland they so desperately desired.

The Holy Spirit Prevents Us from Making Bad Choices

Man had made a terrible choice. Even after God destroyed the inhabitants of the earth by water— save his faithful and obedient servant Noah with his three sons and their wives, and whatever was on the ark with them, the genetic evil nature of man followed him. And the curse of Cain continued, falling upon Ham's son Canaan and his descendants. Despite God's favor upon Shem, which would establish his lineage as God's blessed people, mankind still had no savior and no hope.

Even Moses, whom God chose to lead his people out of captivity in Egypt and entrust with his

Law to govern the people, would ultimately fail Him and be prevented from entering the promised land on earth (Numbers 20:12). Sinful man had no way for his sins to be washed away— except by the imperfect blood of animals. The mighty men and women of faith we know so well— Abraham, Sarah, Moses, David— all of them lived under the Old Covenant — could not keep God's Law, and had no savior to cleanse them from sin. They all lived and died without receiving God's permission to go back to their homeland (Hebrews 11:13).

There are only two exceptions recorded in scripture— Enoch and Elijah were both taken up to heaven by God himself (Genesis 5:24 and Second Kings 2:11-12). Knowing that both men were taken up assures us that Zion awaits us.

Generation After Generation Awaited the Arrival of Jesus

DANIEL 7:18 "The saints of the Most High shall receive the Kingdom, and possess it forever."

Since the beginning of Creation— together with His Beloved Son, Jesus, and the empowerment of God's Holy Spirit on earth, God's spoken Word of Power has been a creative force in making the earth yield abundantly so man could enjoy this temporary life here in the flesh (Genesis 1:29).

Hebrews 1:3 tells us that Jesus holds the universe up by His Word of Power. But after Adam's fall from grace, an earth without hope crushed man's ability to be empowered by God's Word. So, from that point in time until Jesus came, Old Covenant people were ineffective in using the Word against evil except through God's personal intervention. Not to say that they did not anticipate the Savior's arrival and the restoration of man's dominion on earth. Daniel 7:13-14 tells us that the prophet saw a vision of the son of man being presented to God the Father, referred to in this passage as the "Ancient of Days".

The Abundant Life Was God's Plan from the Beginning

DEUTERONOMY 28:2 "All these blessings shall come upon you and overtake you..."

God gave Jesus everlasting dominion. He never intended for us to live even temporarily in an undesirable place on earth. God intended for Adam to live forever on earth. He intended for Noah and his family to enjoy divine prosperity after He destroyed Cain's descendants. He intended for Moses to lead his people into their promised land. His intent was always for man to have the best of everything— his rules for righteous living have never changed— He wanted the Old Covenant Generation to live forever on earth in divine prosperity. And except for Adam's fall, and He took down with him not only his generation, but all generations of people who lived after him— which collectively and chronologically can be referred to as all generations before Jesus completed the Old Covenant at Calvary. However, in God's eyes there are only two generations— the Old and the New. We who believe that Jesus Is Lord and abide in Him are the Blessed Generation of the New Covenant in Christ. And we have a Savior in Christ Jesus Our Lord and His assurance as New Covenant believers that He will be with us always (Matthew 28:20), and that He will never leave us or forsake us (Hebrews 13:5). Not only do we have an eternal home to go to in the age to come, but God's Word in Psalm 91 assures us that we have refuge in Zion as our dwelling place in this life. God promises us the security of His presence and eternal love for those of us who choose to *"dwell in the shelter of the Most High and abide in the shadow of the Almighty"* (Psalm 91:1). It's the second part of the verse that many Christians today cannot seem to understand.

Too Many Christians Decide
to Live Without the Anointing

Sadly, many Christians today do not live in victory on earth. Yes, the Holy Spirit resides with all born again Christians, but the abundant life is not possible for Christians who are resting on the laurels that salvation for eternity gives them. I know because I was one of them for many years. I have since learned God had a hedge around me, anticipating my arrival— after my decision to discharge the commission God the Father declared for me in the beginning, to carry out on earth. My reserved chair remained empty at the marriage feast until I really knew who I was, but I had one— I was foreknown, predestined to be created in the image of Christ Jesus, called, justified and glorified (Romans 8:28-30). My arrival in Zion was long expected by the heavenly host.

What Fruit Does God Want to See Us Produce?

PSALM 128:1-2 Blessed is everyone who fears the Lord, who walks in His ways. You shall eat the fruit of the labor of your hands you shall be happy and it shall go well with you.

When it comes to the subject of fruit, the first question we need to ask ourselves is this: what is fruit? Jesus assures us in John 10:9-10 that He is the Door to Zion, that He came to give us an endless bounty of fruit to eat from the abundance in the Garden of Eden, access to the Holy City, even to God the Father— in His throne room; and to give us the abundant life here on earth. The Bible provides us with many examples of how to reap the fruit or blessings of prosperity— sometimes referred to as the fruit of our hands or the fruit of our labors, available to us here on earth as we live the abundant life as joint heirs with Jesus of everything in heaven and on earth (Romans 8:17). In His *Sermon on the Mount,* as recorded for us in Matthew 5-7, Jesus delineates the multi-fold blessings of a life dedicated to God and the work of the Kingdom. In the *Parable of the Sower,* as recorded for us in Mark 4, Jesus promises all New Covenant believers that we can reap a multiple field of blessings, the fruit produced in the hundredfold return and know the secrets of the Kingdom of God if we will but sow the seed of God's Word into our circumcised heart and bear fruit for Him (Mark 4:1-20; Deuteronomy 30:6). What kind of fruit does a circumcised heart bear? faith in God's Word. Faith puts us in right standing with God— our faith produces our righteousness. Remember: faith was credited to Abraham as righteousness— He believed God (Galatians 3:6). As Habakkuk 2:4 teaches us, *"The righteous shall live by faith."* So it is with us. When we plant the Word of God firmly in the fertile ground of our circumcised heart, Jesus teaches us in Mark 11:23, *"Truly I say to you, whosoever says to this or that mountain, 'Be taken up and cast into the sea', and does not doubt in His heart, but believes that what he says will come to pass, it will be done for him."* God expects to see faith in His Word produce the fruit of our labors— all the things we hope for. By watering God's Word with our faith, the appearance of all these things on earth evidences our faith at work (James 2:17).

In Galatians 5:22, the Apostle Paul identifies the fruit of the Spirit God wants so much to see reflected in our Christian walk— "Love, joy, peace, patience, kindness, goodness faithfulness, gentleness and self-control— against such there is no law." Remember: these things, fruits that God expects from us, are reflections of who we are in Him. He desires for us to live our lives in such a way that the world will know us by our fruits (Matthew 7:20); and He wants us to multiply this fruit. If we find ourselves lacking in any of these things, we may need to replant the Word in our heart to produce the fruit we lack. When we know we are not producing what God expects of us, it's time to decide a thing. The problem: the cares of this world and the desire for other things probably caused us to go astray. We will probably need to plant more Word seeds.

God's Love for Us Is Greater than Anything Known to Man

SONG OF SOLOMON 8:7 Many waters cannot quench love, neither can floods drown it.

All Christians are entitled to citizenship in Zion— but we must claim it. Psalm 39:5 tells us that each man's life is but a breath. Some of us may not want to accept this truth, but that doesn't make it any less true. We are here on earth for a purpose that our Father proclaimed for us during the Creation. God does not intend for his Word to return to Him void; but for it to accomplish the thing that He purposed. If anyone of you who is reading this book wants to make a "career change" today because you need more time to serve God, ask Him to extend your days. God can change his mind about the length of our days so that we can complete our work. He did just that for King Hezekiah, giving him fifteen more years because he prayed (Isaiah 38:5). Some disagree with this position. I have even heard preachers say that it was not God's perfect will to extend Hezekiah's life because his son, Manasseh, who ruled Judah for fifty-five years, was the most wicked king who ever sat on the throne. But Second Kings 23:25 tells us that there was no king as faithful to God as Manasseh's grandson, King Josiah, who ruled Judah for thirty-one years— and who turned to the Lord with his whole heart and with all his soul and with all his might, according to all the Law of Moses, nor did any king like him arise after him. God is in the creation and restoration business. Asking God for more years on earth may be what God intended all along.

The Apostle Paul teaches us in I Corinthians 13:13, that faith, hope, and love abide above all other spiritual gifts— these three, but the greatest of these is love. Hope and faith often fail us, but love never fails. Hope is a vision of what we desire; and we rely on the strength of our faith to see what we desire manifested on earth. Faith brings hope to reality. But the world says, "Be real, you can't have that. It's impossible." Too often we give in to our flesh and doubt sets in. And doubt is an instinctively human reaction when we fail to believe that a task assigned to us can be done. We know what the Bible teaches, nothing is impossible with God (Luke 1:37). Too often we do not know how to prosper in the Spirit, and remaining ignorant, lose our reward. In times of trial or temptation, we often forget that we must open our spiritual eyes and ears to receive the thing we hope for and are believing for so that we can stand on this teaching. The longer our physical senses remain in control, doubt and unbelief of God's Word persists, and the greater the likelihood that fear, hopelessness and despair will set in. Ultimately, our physical senses fail us.

Our Physical Senses
Won't Get Us to Zion

A good example of why our flesh won't get us into Zion is found in Matthew 14:22-33. After the 5,000 had been fed, Jesus asked the disciples to go to the other side of the Sea of Galilee while he dismissed the people and went up into the hills to pray, finishing well into the night. Jesus began walking on the water to the boat, but the disciples mistook Him for a ghost and began screaming fearfully. Jesus identified Himself and Peter asked permission to walk out from the boat to meet him. Jesus said, "Come", and Peter began walking. Since the boat had traveled far, wind-driven and tossed about by the waves, Peter probably walked some distance before his flesh said, "I'm afraid; this wind is too strong", and he immediately began to sink. Jesus instantly lifted Peter from the water— but Peter did walk on water.

"The Thief Comes Only to Steal and Kill and Destroy"

MARK 4:14-15 "The sower sows the Word. And these are the ones where the Word is sown along the path; when they hear, satan immediately comes and steals the Word sown in them.

Now let's briefly address the common message of "doom and gloom" we hear preached today from many pulpits— "There are no prophets on earth in this age;" "The gifts of the Spirit have passed away." It is shameful that satan receives so much help stealing the Word from us, killing our joy, and destroying our hope. As the Apostle Paul teaches us in Romans 10:17, *"Faith comes by hearing and hearing by the Word of God."* Yet the devil's workshop seems to be within the church itself. If the Word is not preached, how are God's people to hear? It is no wonder that God's people perish for lack of knowledge (Hosea 4:6). Dare we say for a moment that prophecy is not for today— preachers prophesy every week from the pulpit; and much of it is bad prophecy. We are prophets and we can prophesy in Jesus' name. God the Father is pouring out His Spirit on all flesh today; and our charge to utter His voice in Jerusalem is here on earth today. We must ask the naysayers, "If all of our higher gifts have passed away, what hope of deliverance do the nations of Abraham have in the "here and now"? And if there are no prophets, surely there are no disciples. And with all the miraculous healings taking place today in full gospel churches, do you suppose it's just all a hoax like some pulpits preach it is? If so, we must be living in complete deception, and we *City Dwellers* must ask, "Must the harvest wait until the hereafter to be gathered?" If so, despite what the Word says, Christ Jesus did not come to give us the abundant life in this generation. Lies. Such false doctrine mocks what our Lord Jesus came for and denies that His Word of Power exists. We are not deceived. Our charge is to proclaim the good news of Christ Jesus (Luke 10:1-9).

God's Word must go forth today. Out of our mouths and hearts, God will roar from Zion. So let us be alert and not slumber. Psalm 118:24 tells us, *This is the day that the Lord has made. Let us rejoice and be glad in it.* And God's Word does not change— It is the same yesterday, today and forever (Malachi 3:6; Hebrews 13:8). And as God has declared, *"My Word will not return to Me void— it will accomplish what I purposed and profit in the thing I sent it to do"* (Isaiah 55:11). Nothing has changed. God's Word is still sent out from His headquarters in Zion. God's question to us is the same as with Isaiah, "Whom shall I send, and who will go for Us? (Isaiah 6:8). And Isaiah answered God, *"Here am I, send me, Lord. I will go."* Get ready. He is calling us today.

The Curse of the Law Fell on the Old Covenant Generation

ROMANS 5:18-19 If, because of the one man Adam's trespass, death reigned through that one man, much more will those who receive the abundance of grace and the free gift of righteousness reign in life through the One Man Jesus Christ.

During the Old Covenant, the people would not listen to the prophets. Despite their pleading, and God even allowing Himself to be found by those who did not seek Him and showing Himself to people who did not ask Him to bless them, the people still would not listen (Isaiah 65:1). The curse of the Law hardened their hearts so that few ever heard the voice of God or the message. Adam's disobedience condemned all men and women living under the Old Covenant to death. So God decided that a New Covenant was needed, and sent Jesus out from Zion to earth to break the curse; and, thereafter, the "whosoevers" who believed in Him as the Son of God would receive the Holy Spirit. And those "whosoevers" who sought the Lord in Zion would find Him; and God would send them back to Jerusalem equipped for battle, and would carry the message of redemption, salvation, and the abundant life wherever they were received. The Bible is still the inspired Word of God. The big change now is Christ Jesus, and the power and authority Jesus gave us to carry on the work of the Kingdom. However, now as then, the world will not hear God's message of salvation in Jesus Christ, the message of Christianity. Worse than that, unfortunately, some Christians who have received the gift of salvation will still not listen to the good news of the "Full Gospel". Many poke fun at us, calling us "Holy Rollers", while others mock us. But the Word still must go forth from Zion to Jerusalem. We know what we must do when they reject the Word— clean the dust off of our feet and move on. Sometimes this is very difficult to do— especially in relationships with family and friends. We must decide a thing in every such case. Do we have a vision that we are to be disciples to members of our own family? If so, fine— God will show us the way. He wants to bless us, knows our heart, and always works for good for all who are called by God for service in the Kingdom (Romans 8:27-28).

We Are *City Dwellers*
Doing God's Bidding in Jerusalem

II Corinthians 5:20 We are ambassadors in Jerusalem for Christ Jesus.

We are Christ's ambassadors. We have been designated by Jesus in Zion to be His representatives in Jerusalem to deliver God's message of salvation and redemption. We who dwell in Zion have been commissioned to preach the Word of God in Jerusalem. Throughout the gospel accounts, Jesus demonstrated this same power and authority of the anointing as He blessed and healed the people while He walked the earth. At the Last Supper Jesus declared that we would continue the work of the Kingdom of God, *"He who believes in Me will do the works that I do; and greater things than these will he do, because I go to the Father* (John 14:12). We know that Jesus was declaring the mission He intended for those of us who sojourn on earth today — as well as then, because He specifically included us in John 17:20 as He prayed to God the Father before His arrest, *"I do not pray for these only, but also for those who believe in Me through their word, that they may be one...I in them and Thou in Me, that they may become perfectly one."* Just as Jesus promised in John 14:16, *"I will send you another counselor — the Spirit of Truth, to be with you forever,"* the anointing was given to the Christians of the early church beginning on the Day of Pentecost when 120 believers were gathered together in one accord, including the eleven disciples and Mary, the mother of Jesus. And suddenly the Holy Spirit came upon them and they began speaking in other tongues as the Spirit gave them utterance (Acts 1:14-15; 2:1-4).

The Holy Spirit has fallen on countless thousands of God's people since the Day of Pentecost. Still some Christians believe that our ability to use a blessed prayer language and walk in the higher gifts has passed away. Hardly. We know better, and it is our responsibility to show them and the world that the power and authority of the Holy Spirit is alive today.

"All Authority in Heaven and Earth Has Been Given To Me"

MATTHEW 28:18-20   "All authority in heaven and on earth has been given to Me. Go therefore and make disciples of all nations, baptizing them in the Name of the Father, and of the Son, and of the Holy Spirit, teaching them to observe all that I have commanded you; and lo, I am with you always, to the close of the age."

Traitor satan's dominance over man ended when God in the flesh was crucified at Calvary and forgave all mankind (Luke 23:34). So it was that God in the flesh redeemed us from the curse of the Law forever and avenged Adam's sin by paying the ransom for the lives of all the saints in captivity. The Old Covenant was fulfilled, and the blood of Jesus made it possible for the sins of all of us who came afterward as chosen ones of the New Covenant to be forgiven by our confession and profession of faith in Jesus as Lord. The blood of Jesus became the propitiation for our sins, making

Him our High Priest forever (Hebrews 2:17, First John 2:1-2). No longer would there be a separation between God and man that prevented any of the redeemed from being in the presence of God the Father. As Jesus breathed His last breath on the cross, and said, *"It is finished"* (John 19:30), the curtain of the temple separating God from man was torn in two and many bodies of the saints who had fallen asleep were raised, coming out of their tombs for resurrection (Matthew 27:51-52).

Dwelling in the Most High's Shelter, Walking in His Shadow

PSALM 91:1-2 **He who dwells in the shelter of the Most High, who abides in the shadow of the Almighty will say to the Lord, "My Refuge and my Fortress; My God in Whom I trust."**

Psalm 84:10, *For a day in thy courts is worth a thousand elsewhere,* is one of the most quoted verses of scripture in the Bible. Yet it is so often misunderstood as we attempt to apply its application to our own circumstances today. Jesus came so that we may have life, and have it abundantly — on earth, in the here and now, and in the life to come (John 10:10). Through our faith in Him as the Lord of our life, we are confident of eternal life, but first we have work to do. We have been commissioned. And, because we belong to Him we have victory, will share abundantly in His suffering and His comfort (II Corinthians 1:5). Often this commitment will require us to forego our desire for other things, and perhaps even abandon our associations with close friends and family whose interests are contrary to the perfect will of God. We must remember that we are spirits constantly in need of other spirits who share our desire to fulfill the perfect will of God. To do this, we must spend quality time with God, dwelling in Zion in the Spirit. Jesus declares in Mark 10:30, *"He who has left everything for My sake and follows Me shall receive a hundredfold now in this time..."* This means that we can reap a hundredfold blessing in everything God considers vital to our abundant life on earth. God wants to bless His children in this lifetime. He is a loving God and would not want us to wait until we die on earth to receive His blessings. And we know we are His children because, *"We have received the Spirit of Sonship. When we cry, 'Abba, Father.' it is the Spirit Himself bearing witness with our spirit that we are children of God, and, if children, then heirs of God and fellow heirs with Christ Jesus, provided we suffer with Him in order that we may also be glorified with Him"* (Romans 8:15-17).

Deuteronomy 28:1-14 and Malachi 3:10-12 tell us that our obedience to His perfect will means all the blessings of heaven await us in Zion— Sweet Beulah Land. And Jesus has prepared a place for us there. Ask yourself this important question, since we are God's children and joint heirs with Jesus, would we not want to see them and them us before we die on earth? More importantly, we need to be about our Father's work. So, let's "Mount Up" and "Go Up" into the house of the Lord today, with gladness (Psalm 122:1).

8

Deciding A Thing, A Creation Gift

City Dwellers Can and Will
Make Holy Decisions

JOB 22:28 **You will decide on a matter, and it will be established for you; and light will shine on your ways.**

The gift of deciding a thing is a creation principle God has made available to all His children who live under the New Covenant of Christ Jesus. When we learn to use this principle effectively, we can begin enjoying the abundant life here on earth, and ensure that God's Word does not return to Him void, but accomplishes the thing He purposed it to do and prosper in the thing He sent it (Isaiah 55:11). In the beginning God envisioned a thing, decided He would create it, established the thing, and saw that it was good when it appeared. Throughout Genesis 1, God tells us how He followed this same pattern every time; and, as recorded in verse 31 — the last verse of the chapter, God saw everything that He had made, and, behold, it was very good.

Why is it necessary for us to know how He made heaven and earth, and the hosts of them? Because He wants us to put on and use the creative mind of Christ He gave us to continue working His perfect will (Philippians 2:5, 13). This is what Jesus tells us to do in John 14:12, *"If you love Me, you will do the things I have done. Even greater things than these will you do because I go to the Father."* Here's the thing we must never forget, God created us in His Own image and likeness— and in the image and likeness of His Son, to have dominion over all creatures over all the earth— and He blessed us to be fruitful and multiply (Genesis 1:26-27). Multiply what? We think of propagation— yes, but what about creations and discoveries? What about our works of faith? And what about God's perfect will? God surely want us to be fruitful and multiply all these things.

Binding & Loosing Are
Necessary Decisions

It's easy to dream about being out of debt— or even to visualize it. After all, at one time we were "debt-free". But we dare not visualize being debt-free without being careful to first bind the forces that got us into debt in the first place. This is also a decision— a decision to bind those evil forces, including our own flesh. Surely the devil lured us into his trap by creating the apparition of a shiny new red convertible in our driveway such a delight to our eyes; and the picture of us enjoying all the condo amenities of an expensive beach trip to the fabulous place that our good friends recommended was just too good to pass up. But the devil does not force us to spend the money we need for the mortgage payment and the children's college expenses — our flesh yields to his temptation because we want to keep up with the Joneses; and we convince ourselves that it will be okay to deny ourselves nothing today and pay tomorrow. Face it. It is impossible to visualize the shiny new red convertible in the driveway — or that fabulous beach vacation — until we loose the bonds of any debt that still holds us captive, being sure to also bind the debt demon. Otherwise we are apt to follow an apparition the devil conjures up — or the lustful vision our flesh desires, causing us to discount going God's Way.

Today Is the Day
the Lord Has Made

It's not about paying tomorrow — that mindset is the little fox trying to spoil our vineyard (Song of Solomon 2:15). The battle must be fought today to avoid an even bigger problem tomorrow. This is the day the Lord has made; so let us rejoice and be glad in it (Psalm 118:24). We must bind and loose today. Jesus teaches us in Matthew 6:25-34, *"Do not be anxious about your life — what you should wear or what you should eat or what you should drink. Which of you can add one cubit to your span of life by being anxious about such things? The birds of the air neither sow nor reap yet your heavenly Father feeds and houses them. Consider the lilies-of-the-field and how they grow; they neither toil nor spin. Yet even Solomon in all his glory was not arrayed like one of these. Seek first the Kingdom of God and His righteousness and all these things will be yours as well."*

So, in binding and loosing, we must first bind up things on earth that will hinder us from realizing the vision— at least not in a timely manner; and we must loose good things on earth from where they are being held now by the enemy. Jesus promised us, *"Whatever you bind or loose on earth will also be bound or loosed in heaven"* (Matthew 18:18). We have His Word.

God's Visions vs. Satan's Apparitions

JOHN 10:10   Jesus said, "The thief comes only to steal, kill and destroy; I came that you may have life, and have it abundantly.

Any anointed decision begins with a vision of the thing we hope for. However, when our flesh is in control we become easy prey for satan's counterfeit apparitions. Lest we are careful to use our spiritual senses to see through his apparitions when he confronts us (Hebrews 5:14), we are apt to mistake his warped vision for the real thing. He and his demonic army would like nothing better than to destroy our vision, steal our hope, and kill our decision-making ability. So, when we bind the devil up, we need to exercise our spiritual senses.

Jesus Made a Decision,
He Decided to Die for Us

Believers know that all New Covenant believers are shareholders in the Kingdom of God. This is why we must abide in His words and carry out our commission (Matthew 28:18-20). It is because of our inheritance that we can have the things we hope for— the things we dream of having, the desires of our heart (Psalm 37:4). We can visualize all these things in the Spirit. It is our inheritance (John 16:14-15). Jesus has given us His power and authority to bind and loose (Matthew 18:18). This is why we must exercise our spiritual skills in making *Anointed Decisions* (Hebrews 5:14).

In the Beginning God Decided a Thing

JOB 28:23 God understands the way to wisdom and He knows the place of understanding.

Genesis 1 & 2 tells the familiar story of the Creation from the very beginning. It is an interesting and instructive synopsis of what took place during each of the six days God the Father worked— completing His work and resting on the seventh day from all of His labors, blessing the seventh day and hallowing it because on it He rested (Genesis 2:2-3). We are not sure how long it took God to complete the job— in terms of our time. However, because He made us in His image and after His likeness (Genesis 1:27), we know that He intended to show us "how to" do the things that He did so that we would do likewise when our time came to sojourn on earth. While Genesis 1 & 2 provides us with a good starting point, let us explore further in the Word to get it right. In combination with Genesis 1 and 2, Job 28:23-28 and Proverbs 8:14 gives us a much more complete pattern. When God decided a thing, He followed it all the way through until it was manifest.

We must also realize that God's perfect creation was contaminated by satan and the forces of evil, and completed in perfection when Jesus came to earth in the flesh, was crucified and resurrected. And what remains to be done now is our responsibility. When we have accepted His commission— we are pledging that God's Word which He declared in the beginning will not return to him void; that it will accomplish what He purposed it to do, and that it will prosper the thing to which He sent it (Isaiah 55:11). Then Jesus can return just as He said in Rev. 21:6, *"It is done. I am the Alpha and the Omega, the Beginning and the End."*

God Decided Each Thing
He Created in the Beginning

Therefore, since we are His children, throughout His Word He is showing us "how to do" so that we may be the creative force on earth He intends for us to be. This is why Christ Jesus came to earth, saying to his disciples in John 14:12— yes, that means us, *"Truly, truly, I say to you who believe in Me, you will also do the works that I do; and greater works than these will you do because I go to the Father."* Of course, Jesus was really saying, "Friends, soon I will be going home and won't be here to tell you when and show you how to do everything. But I have shown you the Way and the Truth so that you may see the Light. Remember what I have told you and shown you, and I promise you that the Light will still be with you as you carry out my Father's will. Don't be anxious— you'll do fine— you'll do even greater things than the works you have seen done."

No, Jesus is not here now— in the flesh, but His Spirit is with us. It is important for us to remember that God intends for us to reign in our domain on earth just as He reigns over all of us— and just as His Son—King Jesus, Lord Jesus, reigns in heaven and on earth. For this purpose, Jesus commissioned us in Matthew 28:18-20 to continue God's work— so that whatsoever God decided in the beginning will not return to Him void, but will accomplish that which He purposed it to do and prosper the thing He declared it to do (Isaiah 55:11). After His victory over satan at Calvary but before He ascended into heaven, Jesus passed on to us His power and authority to assure us that He is now fully in charge on earth— satan can no longer make that claim as he did when he tempted Jesus with it while He was in the wilderness, as recorded in Luke 4:1-13. Jesus regained man's dominion on earth at Calvary. We have dominion, but we must exercise dominion, satan has nothing to threaten us with but our own flesh.

We must muster the courage to stay true to our commitment to Him and reign as kings on earth. Jesus explains to us in John 15:14 that we are His friends if we do what He has commanded us to do. We are branches of the tree of righteousness planted by the rivers of living water— yielding fruit in season, ever alive and producing fruit (Psalm 1:3). We have the whole Gospel to share with our lost brethren throughout the nations of Abraham. Jesus has commissioned us all to continue His work on earth, beginning in Jerusalem; and has instructed us to *"shake the dust off your feet"* and move on when the message of the Good News of Christ Jesus we proclaim as His disciples is rejected by a house or town laden with evil (Matthew 10:14). We need not attempt to preach the gospel truth to those who refuse to hear the Word or to skeptics who scoff at it. As we abide in the words and acts of our Lord Jesus, we will be received by the willing.

We Decide a Thing, God Blesses the Thing We Decide

JOB 22:28 "You shall decide a thing and it will be established for you, and light will shine on your way."

So often we hear Job 22:28 preached from the pulpit today, "You shall decree a thing and it will be established for you." But numerous times we fail to hear the last part of the passage— if preached at all, *"...and light will shine on your way."* Job 22:28 is not only Good Word, it contains a commandment— *decide a thing.* When we do, we see. We have a vision and a path to produce what we envision into reality on earth.

9

Trumpet Calls

Listen for the Trumpet Call,
to *Mount Up to Zion*

PSALM 84:5,7 Blessed are we whose strength is in Thee, and in our heart are the highways to Zion...And in Zion we go from our strength to His strength.

Men and women in the armed services learn to listen for and distinguish different trumpet (bugle) calls. Reveille is an early morning wake-up call (of course trainees are usually already well awake, but they play it anyway). There are many other calls— and trainees are required to know the meaning of each call. First Call or Assembly is a call to assemble for morning formation; Retreat, to signal the end of the work day; To the Colors, as a salute to the flag; Taps for lights out; and others of a more routine nature, like Mess Call and Mail Call. Occasionally a Full Dress call sounds in preparation for a parade or celebration.

What Is God Calling Us to Do?

The important thing for us to remember is that we cannot serve God effectively in a world full of evil without training our spiritual ears to hear the sound of the trumpet and for what purpose the trumpet is blowing. If our spiritual senses are "tuned in", we will be able to listen to what God is saying to us, and distinctly hear the trumpet blow in Zion. The keener our spiritual senses, the more trained and willing we are to seek His strength and presence continually (Psalm 105:4) — by first going up to Zion where we go from our strength to His strength — before being sent out from Zion armed with King Jesus' royal power and authority. We learn in I Corinthians 14:8, *"If the sound of the trumpet is indistinct, who will prepare for battle."* It comes down to this: just as an army trainee must listen for and know each bugle call, from early in the morning until late in the evening, we must listen for the sound of the trumpet in Zion. This will require us to put on our spiritual ears. And we have a great advantage even over the disciples of that day — the Holy Spirit residing in us. He wants to teach us the distinct sound of each trumpet call, constantly reminding us that the devil no longer has any authority on earth — Jesus took it away from him at Calvary and gave it to us.

We Must Be Standing on Holy Ground to Hear the Trumpet Call

Indeed, we are blessed with the Holy Spirit's abiding presence. The Holy Spirit resides in us during our pilgrimage here on earth. We hear much about the trumpet call throughout the Old Testament. He knows when we hear the trumpet distinctly, and He determines when we are ready to *Mount Up to*

Zion— and "go up". After we have accepted Jesus as our Lord and Savior— we must constantly be aware of times when our "old man" raises his head, and we begin to "march to our own drumbeat" or get too busy for God. Beware, satan is trying to reestablish a stronghold in our mind and flesh— and we forget that *"We Are Standing on Holy Ground."* It's more than just a beautiful hymn— just as God reminded Moses when He called him to lead His people out of Egypt (Exodus 3:5,10), God's ground is holy. And we can't go up if we neglect this truth. If we are not listening for the trumpet to blow or for the voice of God calling us to action; and if we do not turn aside, we will surely miss Him. Moses saw the burning bush was not being consumed, and he decided to turn aside (Exodus 3:3). Moses heard the call.

We cannot stand on holy ground with our flesh in control. And if we are not standing on holy ground, we cannot inherit the Kingdom of God at that very moment, in the now— in this lifetime. The cost? We could lose our way— wandering about as did the prodigal son (Luke 15:11-32). Worse yet, we could lose the abundant life Jesus came to give us— oblivious to the commission we are to discharge for Jesus.

It is not by coincidence that during His ministry Jesus often went up unto the hills to pray (Luke 6:12). Matthew 5:1 tells us that before He gave the *Sermon on the Mount*, Jesus saw the crowds, went up on the mountain, and when He sat down his disciples came to Him. The Holy Spirit takes us up to the highway to Zion where Christ Jesus meets us and takes us up to Mount Zion where we walk together. I have read Nahum 1:15 many, many times. Yet, it took all these years for God to show me that my daily walk with Jesus up on Mount Zion occurs when I am willing for the Holy Spirit to take me up. To go up is an essential part of our battle training so that we may be grounded in the Word before being sent from Zion back to Jerusalem. Here is an excellent example of the necessity for us to apply the written Word of God to today and especially to our own circumstances. It is easy for us to read and believe that how beautiful are the feet of our Lord Jesus— of the road He walked for us throughout His ministry, and of us walking in the Light of His countenance. But what is God showing us? We are those who preach the good news— we are Jesus' disciples, those whose feet are beautiful— because we are standing on Holy Ground. And as His disciples, our commission includes enabling others to see the light of the world on the path we walk. It is significant that Jesus washed the disciples' feet at the Last Supper. Peter objected, saying that he would never allow Jesus to wash his feet. But Jesus replied, saying, *"If I don't wash you, you have no part in Me"* (John 13:8). What was Jesus doing here?

The reference here is two-fold: (1) our need for righteousness— Jesus desired for them as well as us today to be washed with the waters of righteousness— to make our feet clean and beautiful, without carrying with us the dust of the world— so that we might stand on holy ground before we are sent out into the world, before we accept our commission and embark on our journey from Zion back to Jerusalem, before we preach the good news to the nations. Only in Zion can we have a true mountaintop experience to equip us with our battle armor. We also hear the Master's voice: (2) our call to serve. In Mark 10:45, Jesus teaches us what we are doing as His disciples: *"The Son of man came not to be served, but to serve; and to give His life as a ransom for many."* Washing another's feet is a sincere indication of one's ministry: To serve the children of God.

What Makes Us Good Listeners

MATTHEW 6:33 "Seek ye first the Kingdom of God and His righteousness, and all these things will be yours as well."

PSALM 37:4 "Take delight in the Lord and in His provision, and He will give you the desires of your heart."

It is impossible to place a value on our relationship with Christ Jesus. The value of our gift of salvation and the privilege of spending eternity with Him and our Father in Zion is of infinite value. It is priceless. And to know that Jesus died so that we can experience the closeness of His presence everyday and enjoy the abundant life— on earth, in this age, is almost inconceivable. Sometimes when we are in our prayer closet or in a praise and worship service we become overwhelmed by the glory and the presence of the

Lord knowing He is with us always— just as He promised. Knowing that God is determined that we have all our needs met and to give us the desires of our heart, we almost want to pinch ourselves to make sure what we are experiencing is real. Knowing how to "go up" to Zion— in the Spirit, we learn the meaning of our citizenship in Zion. We hear the sound of the trumpet with our spiritual ears.

Our Salvation Entitles Us
to Hear the Trumpet Now

I CORINTHIANS 14:8 "If the trumpet gives an indistinct sound, who will get ready for battle?"

God never intended to give us salvation for eternity only. Yes, we are saved by the grace of God— and we have a ticket to Zion. And we don't want to wait for the last trumpet call. We are already citizens of Zion. When we earnestly desire to serve God in the here and now, God intends for us to present our body to Him as a living sacrifice (Romans 12:1). Note the word, body. Our spirit is already holy to God because of our profession of faith in Christ Jesus as His Son and our Lord. But our body of soul and flesh must be reprogrammed often and continually cleansed and renewed. God knows this. Through the prophet Jeremiah we know that as our soul seeks God daily as our portion and hope, waiting silently for Him, He is ever faithful and good to us— showing us His steadfast love with new mercies every morning (Lamentations 3:22-23). The sound of the trumpet will always be distinct for believers who hear with spiritual ears.

We cannot hear the trumpet coming from Zion in the natural; and the carnal mind is too busy feeding itself to understand the call. But when we have grown tired of walking in the light of our own countenance we can hear God well in the Spirit— with spiritual senses— like the whistle of an approaching train. And we will recognize each trumpet call.

The Trumpet Call in Zion Is
Our Signal To Do Something

The prophet Joel describes the coming day of the Lord in Joel 2. The trumpet has been blown on Mount Zion and the alarm has sounded (Joel 2:1). And, yes, the sound of the alarm can be heard now throughout Zion and Jerusalem— and in the heavenlies where demons walk. We see the forces of evil at work on earth today. The world surely must wonder why bad things happen to good people. Many good people don't believe in God. Others don't know if He exists or Who He is. But most of us believe that we are in the last days— that God is pouring out His Spirit on all flesh, and we— the children of God, are prophesying, dreaming dreams, and seeing visions (Joel 2:28-29). The prophet Joel declared the sound of the trumpet as a call to action— to stir up mighty men. *"Proclaim ye among the gentiles. Prepare war, wake up the mighty men. Let the men of war come up to Zion. Beat your plowshares into swords, and your pruning hooks into spears. Let the weak say, "I am strong." Assemble yourselves, and come, all ye heathen, and gather yourselves together round about...It is time to "Put in the sickle and gather the harvest." The Lord roars from Zion, and utters His voice from Jerusalem, and the heavens and the earth shake. But the Lord is a refuge and a stronghold to His people. "So you shall know that I am the Lord your God Who dwells in Zion, on My Holy Mountain – Jerusalem shall be holy, and strangers shall never again pass through it"* (Joel 3:9-17). This is our trumpet call. God very much desires for Jerusalem to be holy. Our mission is to rebuild and repopulate Jerusalem as disciples of Christ Jesus.

We Need Zion's Trumpet to Awaken Us Each Day

Jerusalem is where we reside while we are in the flesh on earth. And because we do, our flesh is always trying to find a place to rest, to relax itself. But our spirit man is always alert and raring to go. Maybe that's where we get the expression, "The spirit's willing, but the body is weak." True enough. So, while our flesh sleeps we need a reveille trumpet call each morning to awaken our soul so we can seek the Lord concerning the things that need to be done in that day and be about the

Father's business (Luke 2:49). Jesus teaches us in Matthew 6:31-34, *"Do not be anxious, saying, 'What shall we eat?' or 'What shall we drink?', or 'What shall we wear?' For the gentiles seek all these things, and your Father knows that you need them all. But seek ye first the Kingdom of God and His righteousness, and all these things shall be yours as well. Therefore, take no thought about tomorrow, for the morrow shall take thought for the things of itself. Let the day's own trouble be sufficient for the day."* Proverbs 8:17 confirms this valuable lesson, as we hear the voice of God telling us, *"I love them that love Me; and those who seek Me early will find Me."* The psalmist David also speaks of the need for us to seek God first each day, teaching us in Psalm 63:1, *"O God, thou art my God; early will I seek Thee."* And the prophet Jeremiah, writes in his Lamentations 3:22-24, *The steadfast love of the Lord never ceases, His mercies never end. They are new every morning; great is Thy faithfulness. "The Lord is my portion," says my soul. "Therefore, I will hope in Him."*

"This Is the Day That the Lord Has Made"

Our Jerusalem is our very own mission field where God has assigned us— and commissioned us when we are ready to disciple and baptize the nations of Abraham in His Name. In accepting our commission, not only do we hear Zion's trumpet distinctively with our spiritual ears, we hear the festal shout. Why? Because we have invited His presence; He is with us. It is the Festal Shout we hear and know as we walk in the light of His countenance (Ps. 89:15). Early each morning we need to salute the Father and thank Him for another day to serve Him on earth. This is the day that the Lord has made for each one of us. Let's thank Him for it early each morning, and be about our Father's business (Psalm 118:24; Luke 2:49).

We Hear Zion's Prayer Trumpet

Prayer is two-way communication with the Father— in Zion. So, when we hear the prayer trumpet, we know it's time to go to the altar— whether in the church sanctuary or our own prayer closet. Because we know the way, we can *Mount Up to Zion*. We worship Him in Spirit and truth as we enter into His presence with singing, His gates with thanksgiving and His courts with praise (Psalm 100). At which time we present our petitions and supplications, and listen to what He would have us do for the Kingdom. God inhabits our praise. The Baptism in the Holy Spirit provides us with a prayer language that God understands and satan does not. Our empowerment enables us to *Mount Up to Zion*. We meet with Him in Zion, in the Holy of Holies. In Acts 19:6, the Apostle Paul laid his hands upon a certain group of disciples at Ephesus who had only received John's baptism, and had never even heard of the Baptism in the Holy Spirit. And when he had done so, the Holy Spirit came on them; and they spoke with tongues and prophesied. This was clearly an outward sign of the Baptism in the Holy Spirit providing them with a prayer language. In Ephesians 6:18, as a part of the whole armor of God, Paul teaches us to pray constantly in the language of the Holy Spirit when we are doing battle with satan. Again, this is clearly a call to use our prayer language to communicate with the Father and with Christ Jesus. We may live in two different worlds— but God wants Jerusalem to come home. He refers to us as *My children who dwell in Zion at Jerusalem* (Isaiah 30:19). Remember: each of us dwells in our Jerusalem on earth that God intends to be the image of Zion. He's counting on us to help His Word accomplish His purpose; and He will prosper us as the willing vessel (Isaiah 55:11).

Putting on Spiritual Ears to Hear the Trumpet

The key to our daily communication with God is to put on the mind of Christ— and we can do that more easily when we put on the spiritual senses of our anointing. This is why praying in the Spirit is so important— and why we need spiritual ears to hear and identify trumpet calls from Zion. Such is foreign to our flesh and minds so our soul must be renewed continually. Praying in the Spirit, i.e., praying in our prayer tongue, helps us to hear and distinguish one trumpet call from another. As the Apostle Paul reminds us, praying in our prayer language edifies ourselves; and if a believer is praying in his prayer tongue during public worship, such is not to be confused with offering a prayer in tongues with an interpreter as a function of the gifts of the Spirit for the edification of the body. Therefore, praying in one's prayer tongue while in public worship should not disturb another believer's worship. However, words of prophecy, knowledge and wisdom in the language of our understanding may be given in public worship (I Corinthians 14:14 & 12:10). Therefore, when we hear the sound of a trumpet and can identify the call, it would be very appropriate to share the meaning of the call with the church body as a word of knowledge as we should upon seeing a heavenly vision, smelling a pleasant aroma, or feeling the Holy Spirit falling upon us, we should share such with the church body as a testimonial to glorify God.

Remember, brethren, when we are in the Spirit, demons cannot be present nor can they intercept our communications with Him— because we are already in Zion. That's right. When we pray in the Spirit, we let go of our physical surroundings, whether we are in our prayer closet or the church sanctuary, and we surrender completely to the Holy Spirit. He will carry us up to Zion. All we really have to do is ask Him to transport us, and allow Him to do it. And, yes, He can take the whole body of the church up to Zion as our flesh is slain in the Spirit.

A Distinct Trumpet Sound Can Only Be Heard with Spiritual Ears

I CORINTHIANS 14:8   If the trumpet gives an indistinct sound, who will be ready for battle?

The more we pray in the Spirit, the more we hear the sound of the trumpet; and the more often we can experience Zion as our homeland and our life there as *City Dwellers*. It only gets better, because the closer we move to the Father's throne room in Zion the clearer we hear the voice of God— and the sound of the trumpet gets louder. Hebrews 4:16 urges us to move ever closer to His throne room in Zion, *Let us then with confidence draw near to the throne of grace, that we may receive mercy and find grace to help us in time of need.*

While we should pray with our understanding when speaking in the public arena, we must know that only when we are in the Spirit can we hear God, the Festal Shout (Psalm 89:15), and the trumpet blast with our spiritual ears. The Apostle Paul tells us in I Corinthians 14:8, *"If the trumpet gives an indistinct sound, who will be ready for battle?"* We won't be ready to battle our enemy when we try to live by this world's standards, sending up "arrow prayers" and "help calls" from earth only to have them intercepted and long delayed before reaching the Father. Again, we must be in the Spirit to assure ourselves that our prayers will be promptly received and that we will hear communications from Zion.

Out of Zion's Hill
Salvation Has Come

Doing the world's business often hinders us from understanding and acknowledging the power and authority of the Holy Spirit's anointing within us. The demands of our flesh will never allow us to hear the trumpet call in the natural. Our flesh cannot accept that the Baptism of the Holy Spirit has empowered us to accept the Great Commission Jesus gave us in Matthew 28:18-20 *"to go forth from Zion and disciple all nations,"* and will fight in every way possible to disprove the vision. To our flesh, salvation and deliverance have no meaning. But our soul can be trained to listen to the sound of the trumpet. Our spirit man has very good spiritual ears. We have work to do today. We know that the nations of Abraham, all together as one in their Christian faith— in their obedience to God's Word, await our arrival. We chosen ones are coming to set the nations free from bondage. We are the ones who are coming out of Zion's hills to bring hope to the nations. In Genesis 12:1-2, God called Abraham and told him to go for Him, saying, *"Go from your country and your kindred and your Father's house, and I will make of you a great nation."*

Of course, we know Abraham as the "Father of Many Nations". In reality, God is referring here to the tie that binds us together as one in Him. We are all one nation of New Covenant believers in Christ. As we revisit the Last Supper, we again hear our Lord praying the Father, *"I do not pray for these (eleven) only, but also for all those who believe in Me through their words; that they may all be one; even as Thou, Father, art in Me, and I in Thee, that they also may be in Us, so that the world may believe that Thou hast sent Me* (John 17:20-21).

We Are God's Chosen Ones
Coming Out of Zion's Hills

Often we must be reminded of who we are. We have heard the trumpet call. We have been commissioned by God to be prophets to the nations through His inspired Word. Characteristic of the same miraculous movement of the Holy Spirit that existed when God showed himself strong in the Old Covenant among a few anointed prophets and kings He could trust, its message is the same for today. As in the days of David, Elijah, Ezekiel and all the other prophets of the Old Testament, the good news of the New Covenant in Christ Jesus must be carried to the nations. The prophecies in God's written Word were altogether embodied in Christ Jesus; and before He ascended into heaven after His resurrection, He gave the Great Commission to His disciples throughout this age, charging us as His chosen ones on earth today to carry out the good work He started. Through the centuries since Jesus ascended, the Holy Spirit's anointing in Christ Jesus has been passed to His disciples and prophets— and now to our watch in the 21st century. Can't you feel its power moving in and through us? Because of who we are, we are able to hear the trumpet call in the Spirit, and carry His Word of Power to the nations.

We are told by the Apostle Paul in Romans 10:17, *"Faith comes by hearing and hearing by the Word of God."* But verses 14 and 15 tell us how the message of faith gets into the spirit of man: *"How are men to call upon the Name of the Lord to be saved in Whom they do not believe? And how are they to believe in Him of Whom they have never heard? And how are they to hear without a preacher? And how can men preach unless they are sent?"*

We hear this familiar passage repeatedly in full gospel churches today. What we don't sometimes realize is that Paul is talking about us. We are the chosen ones who are commissioned, charged, and sent to carry God's Word of salvation, deliverance, and healing to the nations. The nations include neighbors, friends co-workers, strangers you encounter along the way and your own family.

Blessed Are the Feet of Those Who Go Up

NAHUM 1:15 Behold on the mountains the feet of Him who brings glad tidings, who proclaims peace.

Romans 10 is one of those revelation chapters in the Bible that jumps out at us. Note the second part of verse 15 as Paul quotes Isaiah 52:7, *"Blessed and how beautiful are the feet of those who preach the good news."* This passage is especially significant when we examine two companion scriptures. Nahum 1:15 and Psalm 119:105 both teach us about the steps our feet trod. We can imagine ourselves in a relay race, and Jesus has just handed us the baton to take His message of salvation and hope for the abundant life to the nations of Abraham. We are expected to run this race to the end, proclaiming the good news of the Gospel. Yes, our feet are blessed and God's Word gives us the light we need to win the race for the sake of all the lost. His Word is a lamp to our feet and a light to our path.

It's all about our Lord Jesus and who we are in Him— as His disciples. We are the Chosen Ones who have heard the sound of the trumpet. So what are we going to do about it? We can never forget why these scriptures are so vitally important to us. We Are *City Dwellers*. We were birthed in Zion, and to Zion we have returned to claim our citizenship privileges— so that we may receive and discharge the Great Commission Jesus gave us. Yes, we have the gift of eternal life given to us by God the Father for our faith in Christ Jesus. Now we can "go up". We can "go up", enter into our Father's throne room by the Door— Christ Jesus, and be strengthened by the armor of God; and we go out again to Jerusalem to declare the gospel, baptize and disciple other Christians so that they too may receive the Baptism in the Holy Spirit. James 1:17 tells us, His light is the precious bounty of the gifts of the Holy Spirit which have come down upon us from the Father of Lights who resides in the Holy City of Zion above. We know that when we lift up our eyes unto the hills our help comes from the Lord of hosts who dwells in Zion above; and He will not allow our foot to be moved (Psalm 121:1-3). But He requires us to first stop living here in Jerusalem by the world's standards. Allow the Holy Spirit to lead us, listen for the trumpet call, and proclaim the Gospel of Christ Jesus.

The Trumpet Calls Us Today to Let God Circumcise Our Heart

When God gave Old Covenant people the Law, He instructed them that He was their one and only God, and that they were to *"love the Lord your God with all your heart, soul and might* (Deuteronomy 6:4-5). But because they could only use their physical senses, they were unable to understand how to circumcise their own hearts so they could receive His blessings and to be no longer stubborn (Deuteronomy 10:16). They continued to be stubborn and self-serving, and thus remained unblessed. Despite having Deuteronomy 28 to tell them how to receive God's blessings or continue living under the curse, they didn't get it. This passage is very familiar to New Covenant Christians, however. God describes the blessings for obedience and the curses for disobedience, and because we are able to understand what the circumcision of our hearts means, all of us should be living according the blessings and not under the curses. This passage is prophecy to us, because when we accept Jesus as our Lord and Savior, the Holy Spirit takes up permanent residence in us. We hear the trumpet call when we make the decision to serve Him only. God circumcises our hearts *(Deuteronomy 30:6).*

Are Our Spiritual Ears Open?

Before our conversion and acceptance of Christ Jesus as Lord, we were just like Old Covenant people— stubborn, unwilling and unable to obey. Our ears were deaf to the sound of the trumpet. Our "old man" was like that; and occasionally he still rears his head. But whatever our own weaknesses prevented us from doing, Jesus made possible. As we open the door to our heart and surrender to God's will, the Holy Spirit lifts us up. Psalm 24:3-7 tells us that all *City Dwellers* can "go up". God the Father has proclaimed this about us: *"Who shall ascend the hill of the Lord? Who shall stand in His holy place? He who has clean hands and a pure heart, who does not lift up his soul to what is false and does not swear deceitfully, he will receive blessing from the Lord, and vindication from the God of His salvation. Such is the generation of those who seek the face of God. Lift up your heads, O gates and be lifted up, O everlasting doors. That the King of Glory — strong and mighty in battle, shall come in."*

The difference in where we were then and now is as light is different from darkness, as hearing is different from deafness. We could see no divine light — we could not hear the sound of the trumpet. But we now have spiritual senses as well as physical senses.

Let the Blessings Flow

Our feet are blessed when we walk in the light of His countenance. Our path is blessed because we see His Light upon our way. Our mission is blessed because we comprehend it. Our Christian walk is blessed because we have a vision of what we see in the Spirit. But our acknowledgement to God that His Word is a *lamp unto our feet and a light unto our path* (Psalm 119:105) should be declared in conjunction with verse 106 — as a sworn oath, a statement of our belief, to be confirmed daily. His Light is ours because we have declared it so— and because of our sworn profession of faith in Christ Jesus and obedience to His Great Commandment— "To love God with all my might, heart, understanding, soul, and spirit— and my neighbor as myself" (Mark 12:28-31). We hear the trumpet calling us to take our position against the enemy; and we hear the trumpet declaring our victory— through our Lord Jesus.

What Does "Seal Us O Holy Spirit" Mean for Us?

The anointed words of an old hymn, *Seal Us O Holy Spirit*, is what God wants to do for believers today. When we are sealed by the Holy Spirit, we understand that the New Covenant represents the body of Christ Jesus in us and His blood shed for our redemption. When Jesus baptizes us in the Holy Spirit, we receive gifts of the Spirit, as God determines, empowering us in the same manner Jesus Himself was empowered. God wants to hear each of us proclaim the new creation in us as we worship and praise Him, and as we teach and preach the Gospel.

The Devil Can Defeat Us When We Battle Him in Our Flesh

Equipped with the wisdom and insight of the Holy Spirit, we should be able to stand against the forces of evil at work on planet earth— i.e., if we are dressed in our full battle armor— including praying at all times in the Spirit (Ephesians 6:18).

301

But the Apostle Paul warns us to put on the mind of Christ (Philippians 2:5). Again in Colossians 3:2, he instructs us to set our minds on things that are above, and not on things that are on earth. For as Proverbs 23:7 tells us plainly, *as a man thinketh in his heart, so he is.*

Our Lord Jesus Won the Victory for Us at Calvary

We must be able to use our spiritual senses instead of our physical senses if we are to effectively stand against evil. Remember, satan can defeat us if we operate in the flesh— with our physical senses. But we always win when we are in the spirit realm. So why do we Christians fail to use our spiritual senses? Perhaps some of us who say we are filled with the Spirit have never really been baptized in the Spirit. Maybe some of us who know we have received the Baptism forget the importance of this great gift and try to handle the battle in our own way. Maybe we fail to put on our armor. Do we sometimes forget or even deny that we are teachers commissioned by Jesus? Do we dare to have it both ways— trying to serve two masters, still carrying chaff with us? All such conditions result in our failure to serve God.

When Our Abundant Life Is "On the Line", Will We Hear the Call?

For many years during my career as an educator, I coached high school football, basketball and baseball— and before that as a volunteer in youth leagues. One lesson I learned early on— good teams practice well. Teams must be prepared for the battlefield— mentally, physically, emotionally, and spiritually. Games are not so much won and lost on the field of play as on the extent of their preparation before game time. As Hebrews 5:12-14 puts it about those of us who desire to be Jesus' disciples but sometimes we are ill-prepared for the weariness of the fight, by this time we all ought to be teachers— yet why do we need someone to teach us again the first principles of God's Word? We still need milk and not solid food, for we are not mature but remain as children who must be milk-fed and trained by practice to distinguish good from evil.

What a vulnerable and useless state of readiness. We better know evil when we see it— and be prepared to battle against our own flesh, no matter how sweet the voice of evil (Proverbs 9:14-18). The trumpet is calling us to battle. We must learn to listen and distinguish all of our trumpet calls. Evil can often appear to be a wolf in sheep's clothing: She sits at the door of her house, she takes a seat on the high places of town, calling out to those who pass by— who are going straight on their way, saying, *"Whoever is simple, turn in here." And to those who have no (spiritual) sense, "Stolen water is sweet, and bread eaten in secret is pleasant."*

Our Baptism by Fire Is a
Precondition of Discipleship

ISAIAH 43:1-3   Thus says the Lord, He who created you, O Jacob, He who formed you, O Israel. "Fear not for I have redeemed you; I have called you by name, you are Mine.   When you pass through the waters I will be with you; and through the rivers they shall not overwhelm you; when you walk through fire, you shall not be burned, and the flame shall not consume you. For I am the Lord your God, The Holy One of Israel, your Savior."

When we think of the baptism by fire, we should regard it as our total surrender to the perfect will of God. God wants to send us out from Zion to teach the children of God, preach the good news of the Gospel of Jesus Christ and the Kingdom of God, declare His healing power— and to baptize.   But our battle armor must be appropriate for our mission lest our enemy finds a chinch in our battle armor and renders us useless to help the very ones He has called us to disciple. God knows this and will not risk His Word returning to Him void. So before we can expect God to send us to do His bidding and use us effectively on earth, we must be baptized by fire. It is a part of our justification— not as required to receive the gift of salvation, given freely by God the Father to all professed believers in Jesus as Lord, lest any man should boast. But our justification is a precondition of discipleship for whosoever would follow Him today as a disciple of our Lord— to serve the Kingdom. Enduring the devil's temptations without yielding is the baptism by fire required of all of us whosoevers.

Jesus Had No Chaff,
Yet, He Accepted His Baptism by Fire

Our baptism by fire is ongoing— requiring us to continually burn off the chaff during our trial. We need to look to Jesus. He is the Pioneer of our faith (Hebrews 12:2); and even He was required to be baptized by fire. Ours could happen in weeks, but most likely it will take years. Each step we take forward deepens our commitment and strengthens our confidence. We need the Baptism in the Holy Spirit and the higher gifts of the Spirit to complete our battle armor. Going up to Zion is a privilege of our citizenship. God knows we need to be in Zion to recharge our anointing and empower us to stand fast against the forces of evil. And unless the fire has consumed the chaff that causes us to revert back to our "old man" way of thinking and bad carnal habits, we will surely be double-minded— therefore, unstable in all our ways; and we should not suppose that God would give us anything (James 1:7-8). We must endure this trial.

Our Training Begins When
Our Baptism by Fire Is Launched

We may feel like we are armed with the armor of light, that evil cannot penetrate and we can "walk on water" when we first receive the Baptism in the Holy Spirit— but our real training is only beginning. As we allow ourselves to experience the spiritual realm more with each passing day, we know that we dwell in Zion— now; and, from there, we sojourn here in Jerusalem. It's not the other way around.

Each time we are translated in the Spirit of God, we are carried by the Holy Spirit to Zion where we meet our Lord Jesus, who opens the door to our Father's throne room (John 10:9). There we converse with them; and receive strength and instruction before we return to Jerusalem— to minister in Jesus' name; bring the good tidings from Zion to Jerusalem; teach and preach the Gospel; proclaim and publish peace, salvation, liberty to the oppressed; heal the nations of Abraham; and communicate the Baptism in the Holy Spirit to all who desire to receive it. This is our calling. Most of us can remember occasions when our own parents were so well pleased and proud of our accomplishments— whether it was earning a certificate for completing the catechism, making the honor roll, doing well on the athletic field, winning an award, or graduating from high school or college— their joy was always complete. My two brothers and I were their very special sons (no sisters, however). As a career educator, I never met a parent who thought that their children were just "average" or anything other than "special".

Those of us who are parents have always rejoiced in the accomplishments and recognitions of our own children.

Likewise, infinite times over, try to imagine what God the Father felt as He watched His only Son grow into manhood. God knew when Jesus was ready for His baptism by fire and His glorified ministry on earth. Now encased in a body of flesh, God had watched His Son who had helped Him from the beginning grow into manhood on earth. Now His only begotten Son was about to embark on a three-year journey that would cost Him His life but save mankind. Imagine what God was feeling as He anointed His Beloved Son, Jesus and filled Him with His Holy Spirit—and readied Him fully for His ministry, sending Him into the wilderness to be tempted; and out into a cruel world— to save mankind, redeem us from the curse of Adam, and establish the New Covenant with all believers by His Own blood. Surely we can feel what He felt as we hear God the Father say, *"This is My Beloved Son of Whom I am well pleased."* We all know what happened next. Armed with the whole armor of God and of light, Jesus resisted all of the devil's temptations. In the Spirit, Jesus kept satan at bay.

In every aspect of the Christian walk Jesus established the pattern for us to follow in His footsteps. Hebrews 12:2 tells us that Jesus is the Pioneer and Perfecter of our faith. Before we can preach the message of salvation to the nations—the message that frees God's people from bondage, God must know that we first must be equipped with God's whole armor— and that He can trust us under fire. He allows our tests to ready us for battle.

Our Power Comes from
Our Anointing in the Holy Spirit

ACTS 1:8 "You shall receive power when the Holy Spirit has come upon you..."

When Jesus prayed the Father for Him to send the comforter, the Spirit of Truth (John 14:16-17, 26), He knew that His beloved eleven disciples, as well as all others in the early church— including those of us who would follow after them, would need the anointing— i.e., the power of the Holy Spirit working within each of them to prevail against evil in the world. The Holy Spirit is His rod of power working in us. If we look intently at our outstretched hand, we may be able to visualize the rod in our hand.

We know what Jesus intended when He prayed the Father on our behalf at the Last Supper and what He still intends for us serving Him on earth today: to have the same power and authority as the eleven, and that we all be one in Him and the Father because of our confession of faith, the word of our testimony— and His prayer in John 17:20-21. Our Redeemer, Christ Jesus, knew that all of His disciples who were to serve Him during the New Covenant Age would need the power of the Holy Spirit's anointing— in addition to His staff of authority, given to us as citizens of Zion by God the Father, as a component of our redemption. It is up to each one of us to claim and proclaim all of our spiritual gifts, beginning with our gift of salvation unto eternity, and also including:

(1)　　Baptism in the Holy Spirit, with the evidence of praying in tongues (Acts 19:6; I Cor. 14:12 and 15; Eph. 6:18);

(2)　　The Whole Armor of God (Eph. 6:11-18);

(3)　　Gifts of the Spirit (I Cor. 12:1-11);

(4)　　Ministerial Gifts (I Cor. 12:28; Eph. 4:8-11).

We Are Different Parts of the Body of Christ

While we know that we are all different parts of the body of His church with different functions, corporately we know that we are one in Him and the Father (John 17:21-23). Acts 1:8 clearly tells us that the Holy Spirit has come to earth to inhabit us and empower us severally to carry out each of our assigned ministries in His church, representing the different parts of the body of Christ needed to effect the perfect will of God on earth. For this purpose the Father wills that all citizens of Zion— meaning us, receive the Baptism in the Holy Spirit and the special anointing needed to complete our responsibilities on earth in victory so that His Word does not return to Him void (Isaiah 55:11). And by the anointed power of the Holy Spirit as He awakens our spiritual senses, we will know how to *"Mount up on wings as eagles"* and fly away to Zion now, in this age— to be with the Master— our Bridegroom; to receive our Father's counsel. Zion can be ours, now — because we are citizens of Zion. We are *City Dwellers*. And we can have a taste of the Age of Jubilee now, in this New Covenant Age,

10

The Age of Jubilee

ACTS 17:28-29   In Him we live and move, and have our being; as even some of your poets have said, "For we are indeed His offspring." Being then God's offspring, we ought not to think that the Deity is like gold, or silver, or stone, a representation by the art and imagination of man.

Jesus teaches us in Luke 15:7, *"I say unto you, that there will be more joy in heaven over one sinner who repents, more than ninety-nine righteous persons who need no repentance."*   We are the spiritual offspring of God the Father, the Son, and the Holy Spirit.   It is no wonder that our Father wants us back home where we belong.   Each one of us has been sent to earth on a mission for Him — he expects us to complete our mission and return home thereafter.   In the meantime, He expects us to return frequently for visits with Him and our elder brother, Christ Jesus — who just happens to be our spiritual husband and best friend.   This is why each time we return home it is an occasion for us to have a time of joyful glee — like it was in the year of the seventh Sabbath to the Israelites, a year of rest for the land when the land would provide meat for all the people.   And when we complete our mission on earth, it will be like unto a perfect 50th year, a Year of Jubilee, as described in Leviticus 25:11-13, a time when all God's people rested — not continually sowing, reaping, and gathering. They rested. Now, if we could multiply that celebration 100-fold for every 50th year since God made the first man Adam, and reinvested our return every year, the result would be incalculable. We still could not possibly imagine what blessings God has stored up for us in Zion.

Truly, when our mission has been completed here, we can surely experience the Age of Jubilee in the age to come. It will be a glorious day. When He created our spirit man, God gave us part of Himself. We were created in His perfection, He gave us a perfect soul, but, because it was necessary for us to live on earth, God made us a body of flesh from the dust of the earth to house our perfect spirit and soul. Our spirit man is made of the same spiritual substance of our Father God and Christ Jesus.

God fully intended for the first man Adam to live forever, placed him in a garden of plenty, and gave him dominion over all things that moved upon the earth as well as the birds of the air and the fish of the sea. But Adam and his wife Eve disobeyed God, ate of the forbidden tree of the knowledge of good and evil, allowing satan to become their god. From that moment, mankind came under Adam's curse, with no hope of redemption. God banished Adam from a life of abundance, and the entire Old Covenant Generation became a lost generation— separated from the Father forever. But God, in His love and mercy, sent His Son Jesus to earth, to redeem man from the curse and make a way for all mankind to inherit eternal life. When Jesus defeated death at Calvary, He made it possible for all men to be free from the curse of Adam and the Mosaic Law.

The Return of the Prodigal Son Represents a Choice for Us

Each of us is like unto the story of the prodigal son. The earth has been contaminated from the moment Lucifer and his demonic angels were cast out of heaven. When the young son decided to go his own way, out of his father's presence and loving care, he became contaminated and entangled in the ways of a sinful world. But after he returned, begging forgiveness for leaving his father and throwing his life away, his father forgave him, dressed him in fine clothes, and gave him his signet ring.

Christ Jesus Is Our Signet Ring

We have Christ Jesus as our signet ring. And he promises to never let go of our hand. Brethren, the Age of Jubilee will be more than we can ever imagine; and a taste of it is available to us today. We are *City Dwellers*— and we can and shall *Mount Up to Zion* today. The abundant life on earth can be ours. And every year can be a Year of Jubilee as we experience a hundredfold return, not just in one year as did our forefather Isaac— but in every year. As the prophet Isaiah prophesied (Isaiah 64:4), and the Apostle Paul writes in I Corinthians 2:9-10, *"As it is written, what no eye has seen, nor ear heard, nor the heart of man conceived, for those who love Him. But God hath revealed them unto us by His Spirit: for the spirit searcheth all things, yea, the deep things of God."* Amen

Father,

Thank you for this message. I humbly ask you to bless the reader with the abundance of this life, and with all the rights and privileges of citizenship in Your Holy City of Zion. May the reader enjoy Your presence in the Throne Room every morning.

You graciously gave me the inspiration to write this book; and to show all city dwellers that Jesus made it possible at Calvary for the redeemed to "GO UP" to Zion, receive Your strength, come out again and find good pasture in their Jerusalem. Thank you, Father, for Your bountiful inheritance that we may enjoy on Your Holy Mountain.

Cause this book to help each and every reader use spiritual senses daily to exercise dominion on the earth, and enjoy victory over evil in this life now. Father, cause the reader to hear and understand Your Word and enlighten them to Your truths.

Your Word promises that anything I ask in the Name of Jesus that You will do. So I ask all the above in the Name of Jesus, my signet ring.

Ernest Stokes

Made in the USA
Middletown, DE
26 July 2017